The YOUTH VOLLEYBALL Handbook

Master the Basics, Elevate Your Skills,
and Develop Winning Strategies
to Excel on the Court

Pathways Press

TABLE OF CONTENTS

INTRODUCTION:
WELCOME TO THE VOLLEYBALL COURT

Hey there, future volleyball star! If you're reading this, you've already taken the first brave step on an incredible path. And that's what volleyball really represents—a path of growth, not simply a destination.

The reality of volleyball includes messy moments, challenging situations, and sometimes, downright frustrating games. You'll miss balls. You'll serve into the net during game point. You might even wonder why your arms are a little sore and speckled after practice. And yet, something magical happens when six people come together on a court, connected by nothing but trust, communication, and a shared goal.

The truth? Volleyball extends beyond mastering the perfect serve or executing a killer spike. Those skills matter, certainly. But beneath the surface of every great volleyball player lies something deeper: the courage to be seen missing a play, the resilience to shake it off, and the vulnerability to try again—in front of teammates, coaches, and sometimes a gym full of people.

WHY THIS HANDBOOK EXISTS

This handbook emerged from a fundamental belief: Volleyball, at its core, represents one of the most powerful tools we have for developing not just athletic skills, but the human skills that matter most in life. Consider this: Where else might you practice real-time communication, split-second decision making, and emotional regulation, all while trying to prevent a ball from touching the ground?

As volleyball continues to flourish, more young athletes discover what the volleyball community has recognized for decades: This sport transforms lives. From the shy player who finds their voice calling for the ball to the natural athlete who learns that teamwork exceeds individual talent, volleyball has a remarkable ability to meet you exactly where you stand while gently guiding you toward who you might become.

HOW TO USE THIS BOOK

This handbook functions much like a volleyball rally: building progressively, with each skill connecting to the next. You might feel tempted to turn directly to the attacking chapter (everyone loves to hit!), but consider this crucial advice: The foundations truly matter.

Whether you identify as a complete beginner wondering which end of the court serves which purpose or a club player aiming to refine your jump serve, this book contains valuable information for you. Feel free to dog-ear the pages. Write notes in the margins. Take it with you to practice. This book serves not as a pristine textbook but as a working document intended to evolve alongside you.

Parents: This resource is for you, too. Understanding the game your child loves means more than knowing the score—it allows you to speak their language and support their passion.

Coaches: View this as a companion to your wisdom. The drills, progressions, and teaching points outlined throughout these pages aim to complement what you currently implement in your gym.

THE VOLLEYBALL MINDSET

Before exploring the technical aspects, consider this essential truth: Volleyball will humble you—repeatedly. Even Olympic gold medalists shank passes and miss serves. The difference doesn't lie in never failing. These athletes have learned to appreciate the process so thoroughly that failure simply represents another data point.

As you begin your volleyball practice, I offer this promise: When you bring your whole heart to this game—your enthusiasm, your frustration, your determination, your questions—volleyball will provide so much more than merely athletic skills. It will offer you community, identity, and a laboratory for life's most significant lessons.

The court awaits. Your volleyball story begins now.

CHAPTER 1:
VOLLEYBALL FOUNDATIONS

Consider this observation: Volleyball contains wonderfully unusual elements.

Think about what volleyball entails. We've created a game where the primary goal involves preventing a ball from touching the ground by hitting it with our forearms (ouch), we rotate positions like some elaborate square dance, and success often requires throwing your body onto the floor with reckless abandon.

And yet, millions of us around the world remain completely captivated by this beautiful, strange game. So, before examining the technical aspects of volleyball, we should understand the deeper motivations behind the sport.

A BRIEF, SLIGHTLY QUIRKY HISTORY OF VOLLEYBALL

Volleyball was invented in 1895 by William G. Morgan, a YMCA physical education director in Massachusetts. His original goal was to create a less intense alternative to basketball for his older business members. He called it "mintonette," which, thankfully, didn't stick.

Imagine the conversation:

"What sport do you play?"

"I'm a mintonette player."

"A what now?"

The game was renamed "volleyball" after someone noticed players were volleying the ball back and forth over the net. Revolutionary naming process, truly.

What started as a gentle game for businessmen has evolved into one of the most dynamic team sports on the planet, played by over 800 million people worldwide. From the beaches of Brazil to the Olympic arenas of Tokyo, volleyball has morphed and adapted while keeping its core principles intact.

THE COURT: YOUR NEW HOME

A volleyball court is 60 feet by 30 feet, divided by a net whose height varies by age and gender. If that means nothing to you, think of it this way: It's big enough that you'll definitely get your steps in, but small enough that you can't hide from the action.

The court is divided into six zones, numbered in a counterclockwise direction starting from the right back position. Learning these zones is like learning the addresses in your neighborhood—eventually, you'll navigate them without thinking.

But here's the beautiful complexity: While you start in a specific position, once the ball is served, you can move anywhere! This organized chaos is what makes volleyball such a beautiful blend of structure and creativity.

THE POSITIONS: FINDING YOUR VOLLEYBALL IDENTITY

Volleyball has six positions, each with its own personality and purpose:

1. **Setter**: The quarterback of volleyball. Setters touch the ball more than anyone and make split-second decisions that determine the entire offense. Setting might be your calling if you're detail-oriented, love being in control, and have a slightly unhealthy need to orchestrate everything around you.

2. **Opposite/right side**: The volleyball Swiss Army knife. These players must block well, attack from the back row, and handle tough serves. If you're adaptable and have a knack for doing the unexpected, this position has your name on it.

3. **Middle blocker**: The unsung heroes of volleyball. Middles are typically tall, quick, and definitely brave. They rarely get the glory, but they prevent the other team from getting it, too. If you take pride in shutting people down and don't need constant validation, welcome home.

4. **Outside hitter**: The volleyball equivalent of the lead guitarist. They get lots of sets, must pass well, and often have a flair for the dramatic. If you're equally comfortable being the hero or digging a tough serve, this might be your spot.

5. **Defensive specialist**: The volleyball utility player. These athletes sub in for front-row players in the back row and specialize in passing and defense. This role will

speak to you if you're reliable, consistent, and take pride in the perfect pass.

6. **Libero**: The defensive specialist in the differently-colored jersey. Liberos are typically shorter, lightning-fast, and possibly part cat based on their reflexes. If you love frustrating hitters and don't mind sacrificing your body regularly, this is your spiritual home.

Remember: Where you start isn't where you'll necessarily end up. Many of the greatest players in history switched positions multiple times before finding their perfect fit.

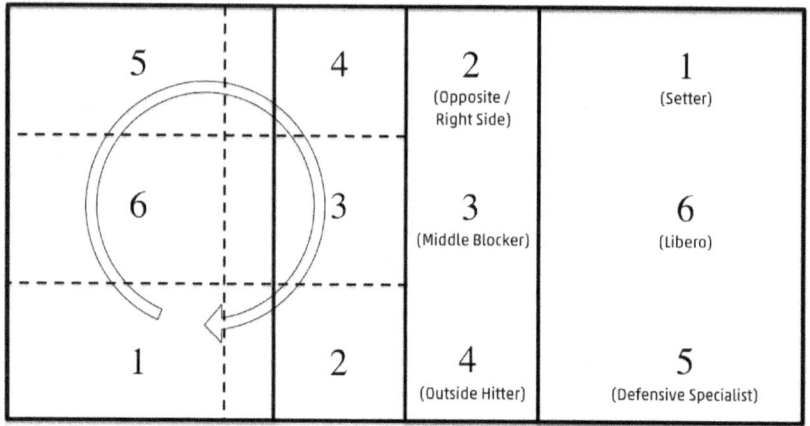

THE RULES: MAKING SENSE OF THE MADNESS

Volleyball rules can seem like someone threw spaghetti at a wall and called whatever stuck "official." But there's method to the madness, I promise.

The basic goal is simple: Get the ball to hit the floor on the opponent's side of the net while preventing them from doing the same to you. Each team gets three touches to make this happen, and the same player can't touch the ball twice in a row (except on a block).

Games are typically played to 25 points (win by 2), and matches are best of 3 or 5 games, depending on the level. Rotational rules ensure everyone gets a turn in each position, which is volleyball's way of ensuring you can't hide in the corner if you're having a bad day.

The scoring system has evolved over time. Back in the volleyball stone age (pre-1999), you could only score points when your team was serving. Now, with rally scoring, every play results in a point for someone. This change is why matches no longer take seventeen hours to complete.

THE EQUIPMENT: VOLLEYBALL'S SHORT SHOPPING LIST

The beauty of volleyball is its simplicity. You need only this:

- **A volleyball**: Preferably one that doesn't hurt your arms too much. Size 5 is standard for ages 13+, with lighter volleyballs available for younger players.
- **Appropriate footwear**: Court shoes with good lateral support are ideal. Running shoes are a common mistake; they're designed for forward motion, not the side-to-side movement volleyball demands.
- **Knee pads**: Are they technically optional? Yes. Will you regret not wearing them the first time you dive for a ball? Also yes.
- **Comfortable athletic clothes**: Nothing too baggy (it can interfere with your movement) or too restrictive (volleyball requires a full range of motion).

That's it! No bats, sticks, racquets, or complex protective gear. Just you, a ball, and the willingness to look slightly ridiculous diving across the floor.

THE VOLLEYBALL MINDSET: WHERE THE MAGIC HAPPENS

Volleyball is 90% mental. The physical skills matter, of course, but what separates good players from great ones is what happens between their ears.

Volleyball requires a unique psychological profile:

The Courage to Fail Publicly

Every volleyball error happens in plain view. Miss a serve? Everyone saw it. Shank a pass? Can't hide that. Get blocked? The entire gym just witnessed it.

This visibility means volleyball players must develop what I call "failure resilience," the ability to mess up spectacularly and then immediately reset for the next play. This isn't just a volleyball skill; it's a life superpower.

Interdependence: The Sweet Spot Between Dependence and Independence

Volleyball is the ultimate team sport because it forces interdependence. You literally cannot do it alone; the three-touch maximum ensures that. Yet each player must also take complete responsibility for their specific role.

This balance—being both self-sufficient and completely team-oriented—creates a unique dynamic where the whole truly becomes greater than the sum of its parts.

Present-Moment Awareness

Volleyball happens *fast*. A spike can travel over 80 mph, giving you milliseconds to react. This requires what mindfulness experts call "present-moment awareness," the ability to be fully engaged in what's happening right now, not dwelling on the last point or worrying about the next one.

Volleyball players who master this skill often find it transformative in other areas of life, from academics to relationships. Even Karch Kiraly has misjudged serves. The difference is, he recovered—fast.

MODERN VOLLEYBALL: A GAME IN EVOLUTION

Volleyball today barely resembles the gentle game William Morgan created. It has become faster, more powerful, and more specialized with each passing decade.

The modern game emphasizes:

- **Speed**: This is both in terms of quick attacks and rapid defensive transitions.
- **Power**: Jump serves and attacks that were once rare are now standard.
- **Specialization**: Players focus on specific positions earlier, developing deeper skill sets.
- **Analytics**: Data now informs everything from lineup decisions to in-game strategy.
- **Globalization**: Techniques and strategies flow freely across countries and continents.

Despite these changes, the essence remains: six players, three touches, one court, and endless possibilities.

THE TECHNICAL EVOLUTION OF VOLLEYBALL

The volleyball of today represents a dramatic technical evolution from its early days. When Morgan first created the game, the techniques were rudimentary: Players simply batted the ball back and forth. The modern game features sophisticated skills that have developed through decades of innovation.

Serving Transformations

The serve has perhaps undergone the most dramatic transformation. What began as a simple underhand motion to put the ball in play has evolved into a powerful offensive weapon:

- **1950s–1960s**: The standard serve remained primarily underhand, with some players experimenting with basic overhand serves.
- **1970s–1980s**: The floating serve gained popularity, with players discovering that removing spin created unpredictable ball movement.
- **1990s**: The jump serve revolutionized the game, with players like Brazilian star Giba demonstrating how a volleyball could be served with the power and spin of a tennis serve.
- **2000s–present**: The hybrid jump float serve emerged, combining the unpredictability of a float serve with the aggressive positioning of a jump serve.

This evolution continues today, with coaches and players constantly refining serving techniques to gain competitive advantages.

Attacking Systems

The offensive strategies of volleyball have similarly evolved from simple to complex:

- **Early volleyball**: Basic high sets to the outside hitter represented the primary attack pattern.
- **Mid-century**: The introduction of quicker sets to the middle expanded offensive options.
- **1970s–1980s**: The back-row attack added another dimension, with players discovering they could attack from behind the 10-foot line.
- **1990s–present**: Complex offensive systems now include combinations, slides, shoots, and other specialized attacks that coordinate multiple players to confuse the defense.

This sophistication means modern volleyball features chess-like strategic elements alongside its athletic demands.

Defensive Innovations

The defensive side of volleyball has kept pace with offensive developments:

- **Early volleyball**: Basic blocking and digging with limited technical sophistication.
- **1960s–1970s**: The development of the forearm pass revolutionized ball control.
- **1980s**: Introduction of specialized defensive positions, including the eventual creation of the libero.
- **1990s–2000s**: Advanced defensive formations and techniques like swing blocking, reading systems, and specialized floor defense patterns.

Today's defensive specialists train in reading attackers' shoulders, arm swing patterns, and even eye movements to anticipate where attacks might land.

VOLLEYBALL CULTURAL IMPACT

Beyond the technical aspects, volleyball has developed rich cultural significance across the globe. Different regions have developed distinctive styles of play that reflect their broader cultural values:

- **Brazilian volleyball** emphasizes creativity, joyful expression, and individual brilliance within team systems.
- **Japanese volleyball** traditionally highlights precision, discipline, and exceptional defensive coordination.
- **Italian volleyball** often features tactical sophistication and strategic innovations.
- **American volleyball** frequently combines physical power with analytical approaches.

These cultural styles continue to influence one another in our increasingly connected world, creating a global volleyball community that shares knowledge while maintaining distinctive regional characteristics.

VOLLEYBALL'S ACCESSIBILITY APPEAL

One reason for volleyball's remarkable global growth lies in its accessibility. Unlike many sports that require extensive equipment or facilities, volleyball can be adapted to numerous environments:

- **Indoor volleyball** requires simply a net, a ball, and a flat surface.
- **Beach volleyball** needs only sand and a net.
- **Park volleyball** thrives in recreational spaces with portable nets.
- **Sitting volleyball** provides inclusive opportunities for athletes with disabilities.
- **Water volleyball** offers a swimming pool variation.

This adaptability allows volleyball to thrive in diverse settings from Olympic arenas to rural villages, urban recreation centers to beachside vacation spots.

YOUR VOLLEYBALL PATH BEGINS NOW

As this chapter concludes and we prepare to explore the physical skills of volleyball, consider this essential truth: Everyone begins somewhere. Every Olympic gold medalist once missed their first serve. Every college scholarship athlete once couldn't distinguish between a forearm pass and a set.

What distinguishes those who excel in volleyball isn't necessarily natural talent (though that certainly helps). Success comes from a willingness to embrace the discomfort of learning, to work through the awkward phase of acquiring new skills, and to find satisfaction in the process rather than focusing exclusively on outcomes.

Moving forward, consider making this commitment: You'll practice patience with yourself. You'll acknowledge small improvements. You'll maintain perspective when things go wrong (and they occasionally will). Most importantly, you'll recognize that volleyball represents more than simply an activity—it becomes an experience you'll treasure, share with others, and ultimately, grow to appreciate deeply.

The next chapter explores preparing your body for volleyball's unique physical demands. But first, perhaps locate a wall and practice bumping a volleyball against it. Though neighbors might observe curiously, remember that every accomplished volleyball player began with those initial, sometimes awkward, contacts with the ball.

A place awaits you on the volleyball court.

THE SCIENCE BEHIND VOLLEYBALL

Understanding some basic scientific principles can enhance your volleyball development significantly. While players don't need physics degrees, recognizing how science influences the game provides valuable insights:

Physics of Volleyball

The flight path of a volleyball obeys fundamental physics laws that affect every aspect of play:

- **Projectile motion** determines how the ball travels through the air when hit at different angles and speeds.
- **Newton's laws of motion** explain why a strong platform position generates better passes than floppy arms.
- **Rotational mechanics** influence how topspin makes the ball drop faster, while backspin causes it to float longer.

- **The Magnus effect** creates the unpredictable movement in float serves as the ball's seams interact with air currents.

Coaches might not use these technical terms, but their instructions aim to help players work with these physical realities rather than against them.

Biomechanics of Volleyball Movement

Volleyball requires sophisticated body movements that follow biomechanical principles:

- **Kinetic chains** describe how energy transfers through body segments—from legs to core to shoulders to arms—during skills like spiking.
- **Ground reaction forces** explain why the most powerful hitters drive forcefully through their legs before jumping.
- **Momentum transfer** illustrates why proper approach timing matters for attackers connecting with sets.
- **Rotational force generation** shows why proper torso rotation creates more powerful serves and attacks than arm strength alone.

Understanding these concepts helps players visualize proper technique and troubleshoot performance issues more effectively.

Psychological Dimensions

The mental aspects of volleyball have become increasingly recognized as critical to performance:

- **Attention control**: learning to focus on relevant cues (the ball, the setter's hands) while filtering out distractions (crowd noise, scoreboard)
- **Emotional regulation**: developing strategies to manage competitive anxiety and maintain optimal arousal levels
- **Team cohesion dynamics**: understanding how trust and communication patterns affect team performance
- **Growth mindset application**: approaching challenges as opportunities for improvement rather than threats to self-image

Elite volleyball programs now frequently incorporate mental training alongside physical practice, recognizing that psychological skills often determine outcomes between evenly matched teams.

THE GLOBAL LANGUAGE OF VOLLEYBALL

Volleyball terminology creates a specialized vocabulary that connects players across cultural and language barriers:

- **A "pipe" attack** refers to a specific back-row play, regardless of whether you're in Brazil or Japan.
- **"Free ball"** universally signals an easy ball coming over the net.
- **"Ace"** celebrates a serve that directly scores across all volleyball cultures.
- **Hand signals** from coaches and players create a silent communication system understood globally.

This shared terminology helps volleyball players connect across national and cultural boundaries, creating a worldwide community united by a common understanding of the game.

LOOKING FORWARD: THE VOLLEYBALL HORIZON

As volleyball continues evolving, several trends suggest where the sport might head next:

- **Technology integration**: Data analytics, wearable performance trackers, and video analysis systems continue transforming training methods.
- **Specialization vs. versatility tensions**: Coaches debate the optimal balance between developing position-specific skills versus creating adaptable all-around players.
- **Global talent distribution**: Increasing international player development creates more competitive parity across nations.
- **Youth development models**: Evolving approaches to long-term athlete development shape how young players enter and progress through the sport.

Throughout these changes, volleyball's core values of teamwork, communication, and resilience remain consistent foundations. The techniques may evolve, but the fundamental connections between teammates continue forming the heart of the volleyball experience.

YOUR FIRST STEP

You've now acquired the contextual knowledge that frames volleyball's fundamental skills. The chapters ahead will guide you through specific techniques, strategies, and training methods that transform this knowledge into practical abilities on the court.

Remember that volleyball mastery represents a gradual progression rather than an immediate achievement. Each contact with the ball offers an opportunity to improve incrementally. Celebrate progress, maintain curiosity, and connect with the volleyball community that surrounds you.

The volleyball court offers a space where physical challenge, mental growth, and social connection intersect beautifully. Your volleyball story begins here—not with immediate perfection, but with the first step on a rewarding path.

The next chapter awaits.

CHAPTER 2:
PHYSICAL PREPARATION AND ATHLETIC DEVELOPMENT

The volleyball court presents a fascinating physical challenge: It asks you to be stable yet explosive, powerful yet precise, reactive yet calculated. All in a space roughly the size of your average living room.

Your body serves as the primary tool for volleyball excellence. While skill development often captures most of our attention, proper physical preparation creates the foundation that makes all technical elements possible. The strongest passing platform means little without the agility to reach the ball. The most technically perfect hitting approach becomes ineffective without the explosive power to elevate above the net.

This chapter explores how to prepare your body for volleyball's unique demands. We'll cover what makes a volleyball athlete's physical needs different from other sports, how to build volleyball-specific strength and movement patterns, and the often-overlooked foundations of athletic health: nutrition, hydration, and recovery.

UNDERSTANDING THE VOLLEYBALL ATHLETE

Volleyball demands a remarkably well-rounded athlete. Let's examine the specific physical qualities that volleyball requires:

Volleyball-Specific Athletic Demands

- **Multi-directional movement**: Unlike linear sports such as swimming or track, volleyball requires rapid movement in all directions: forward, backward, lateral, and vertical. Your training must reflect this omnidirectional reality.
- **Repeated explosive efforts**: Volleyball players perform hundreds of explosive movements in a single match: jumps for blocks, attacks, and serves, along with quick directional changes and acceleration bursts. These movements require not just power but power endurance—the ability to remain explosive throughout long matches.
- **Postural control**: Strong midline stability through your core and torso creates the foundation for proper volleyball mechanics. Every skill—from serving to passing to hitting—depends on core stability to transfer force efficiently.
- **Deceleration capacity**: The ability to safely absorb force when landing from jumps or transitioning between movements proves just as important as generating force.

Athletes with poor deceleration mechanics face higher injury risks.

- **Shoulder stability**: The shoulder girdle handles tremendous stress in volleyball, with overhead movements placing particular demands on the rotator cuff and surrounding musculature. Proper shoulder function requires both mobility and stability.
- **Ankle resilience**: Ankle sprains represent the most common volleyball injury. Building ankle strength, proprioception, and stability significantly reduces injury risk.

Quick Wins for Athletic Development

- Focus on ankle strengthening exercises to prevent the most common volleyball injury.
- Develop core stability for better control during all volleyball movements.
- Work on safe landing mechanics to protect your knees during repeated jumps.

The Athletic Development Progression

Physical development follows an essential sequence that respects your body's natural learning order. This progression builds each stage upon the previous foundation:

1. **Movement quality:** Develop proper movement patterns and body control.
2. **Work capacity:** Build endurance to handle training volume.

3. **Strength:** Develop force production capability.

4. **Power:** Apply strength quickly through explosive movements.

5. **Velocity:** Express power with sport-specific timing and precision.

Many young athletes attempt to skip directly to power and velocity without establishing the requisite movement quality and strength. This approach limits long-term development and increases injury risk. Patience with the process yields superior results.

Mastering this progression directly impacts your ability to maintain proper technique during long tournament days when fatigue typically causes form breakdown.

ESSENTIAL WARM-UP COMPONENTS

The warm-up serves as perhaps the most consistently undervalued element of athletic preparation. A proper warm-up doesn't merely "get you sweating;" it systematically prepares your nervous system, muscle tissue, joint structures, and mental focus for optimal performance.

The RAMP Protocol

The RAMP warm-up protocol provides a systematic approach to preparation:

- **Raise**: Begin by gradually raising your heart rate, body temperature, and respiratory rate. This increases blood flow to muscles, enhances nervous system activation, and lubricates joints. Activities include light jogging or skipping, gentle dynamic movements, and low-intensity footwork patterns.

- **Activate**: Next, activate key muscle groups that volleyball specifically demands, with particular attention to stabilizers that support proper movement. Focus areas include gluteal muscles (often dormant from excessive sitting), core musculature (transverse abdominis, obliques), rotator cuff and shoulder stabilizers, and the foot and ankle complex.

- **Mobilize**: Mobilize joints through active ranges of motion that volleyball requires. Emphasize thoracic spine rotation, hip mobility in multiple planes, ankle dorsiflexion, and shoulder mobility.

- **Potentiate**: Finally, potentiate your nervous system with progressively more explosive movements that prepare for volleyball's demands: increasingly dynamic footwork patterns, submaximal jumps and landings, reaction drills, and brief, explosive movements.

This progression gradually prepares all body systems for optimal performance. An effective volleyball warm-up typically takes 15–20 minutes. It's time well invested for both performance enhancement and injury prevention.

A proper warm-up dramatically improves your first-ball contacts, reduces missed serves, and enables quicker defensive reactions in the early stages of practice or matches.

Sample Volleyball-Specific Warm-Up
For Ages 10–12

Start with these fundamental elements:

- two laps of the court alternating skipping and light jogging
- side shuffling the width of the court (4 lengths)
- high knees and butt kicks for court length (2 each)
- glute bridges (10 reps)
- bird dogs focusing on shoulder stability (8 reps each side)
- monster walks with mini-band (10 steps each direction)
- world's greatest stretch (5 reps each side)
- ankle mobilization in all planes (10 reps each ankle)
- dynamic shoulder circles progressing in size (10 each direction)
- pogo jumps focusing on ankle stiffness (10 seconds)
- lateral bounds with proper landing mechanics (3 each direction)

For Ages 13–15

Add these elements to the ages 10–12 warm-up:

- carioca step the width of the court (4 lengths)
- dead bugs focusing on core control (8 reps each side)
- thoracic spine rotations in various positions (10 reps each position)
- squat jumps at 60% effort (5 reps)

For Ages 16–18

Further enhance the warm-up with these exercises:

- quadruped shoulder taps with core bracing (8 reps each side)
- active hip circles (10 each direction)
- reaction footwork to partner signals (30 seconds)
- approach jump practice with controlled landings (3–5 reps)

If You Only Do One Thing...

- Never skip your warm-up—even a 5-minute abbreviated version is better than nothing.
- Gradually increase intensity rather than starting with explosive movements.
- Include at least one mobility exercise for ankles and shoulders before playing.

The warm-up should become a non-negotiable ritual before every practice and match. Beyond physical preparation, it creates a mental transition into volleyball-specific focus and intention.

A consistent warm-up routine reduces early-game errors and prepares your body for those crucial first few points that often set the tone for the entire match.

FOUNDATIONAL MOVEMENT PATTERNS

All volleyball skills build upon fundamental movement patterns that transfer force effectively. Strengthening these foundational patterns improves on-court performance and reduces injury risk.

The Seven Essential Patterns

- **Squat pattern**: The squat forms the basis for volleyball's vertical explosion. It trains lower body force production, which translates directly to jumping power for attacking, blocking, and serving.

- **Hinge pattern**: The hip hinge underpins the athletic ready position and jumping mechanics. It teaches proper hip-dominant movement that protects the lower back while maximizing posterior chain involvement.

- **Lunge pattern**: The lunge pattern trains unilateral lower body strength and dynamic stability. This directly transfers to defensive movements and lateral transitions.

- **Push pattern**: The pushing pattern develops upper body strength for overhead actions and protects shoulder health. It particularly benefits serving and attacking mechanics.

- **Pull pattern**: Pulling movements balance pushing patterns while strengthening the back body, which helps maintain shoulder health and posture during long practices and matches.

- **Carry pattern**: The carrying pattern develops core stability and shoulder endurance, creating the foundation for extended rallies and matches where postural fatigue often leads to technique breakdown.

- **Rotation pattern**: Rotational patterns develop the coordinated movement chains that transfer force from the lower body through the core to the upper extremities—precisely what serving and hitting mechanics require.

Mastering these seven movement patterns directly improves your ability to maintain proper volleyball technique even during the most intense and extended rallies.

Sample Volleyball Movement Preparation Circuit
For Ages 10–12

Focus on basic movement competency with these exercises:

- assisted squat: 10 reps (using a bench or chair for depth guidance)
- dowel hip hinge: 8 reps (with broomstick along spine to maintain alignment)
- split stance balance: 20 seconds each side (focus on stability)
- wall push-ups: 8 reps (maintain proper shoulder blade movement)
- bent-over band pulls: 10 reps (focus on squeezing shoulder blades)
- bear crawl: 10 steps forward and back (maintaining level hips)

For Ages 13–15

Progress to more challenging movements:

- goblet squat: 10 reps (with light weight, focus on depth and alignment)
- dowel hip hinge: 10 reps (focus on hamstring tension)
- split stance rotations: 8 each side (rotate from hips while maintaining level shoulders)

- push-up progressions: 8–10 reps (modified as needed for proper form)
- bodyweight reverse lunge: 8 each leg (focus on vertical torso)
- tall kneeling band rotations: 8 each side (control the rotation)

For Ages 16–18

Develop more advanced movement capacity:

- goblet squat: 10 reps (focus on maintaining vertical shin position)
- deadlift pattern: 8–10 reps (with appropriate weight for technique)
- quadruped shoulder taps: 10 each side (keep hips completely level)
- push-up with shoulder tap: 6–8 reps (maintain core control throughout)
- bodyweight split squat: 10 each side (focus on knee tracking)
- Pallof press: 8 each side (resist rotational forces while maintaining tall posture)
- wall slides: 10 reps (maintain contact points throughout movement)

Quick Wins for Movement Development

- Practice the hip hinge daily to protect your back and improve jumping mechanics.

- Incorporate rotational exercises to enhance serving and hitting power.
- Master bodyweight control before adding external resistance.

These movement patterns directly transfer to volleyball-specific actions, improving your defensive ready position, attack approach, and ability to quickly change directions during play.

VOLLEYBALL-SPECIFIC STRENGTH DEVELOPMENT

Strength provides the foundation for all power expression. Without adequate strength, explosive volleyball movements become limited regardless of technical proficiency.

Prioritized Areas for Volleyball Strength

- **Lower body strength**: The lower body generates 60–70% of the power in volleyball's explosive movements. Key focus areas include the quadriceps (primary muscle group in jumping actions), posterior chain (glutes, hamstrings—essential for approach acceleration), and calf complex (critical for last-stage jumping power and landing control).
- **Core and torso stability**: The core transfers force between the lower and upper body while providing postural control. Volleyball-specific core training should emphasize anti-rotation strength (resisting unwanted torso rotation during asymmetrical movements), anti-extension control (maintaining proper pelvic position during overhead activities), rotational power (developing

coordinated rotation for serving and attacking), and lateral stability (controlling side-bending forces during lateral movements).

- **Upper body pushing and pulling balance**: Volleyball tends to overdevelop anterior (front) muscles while neglecting posterior (back) muscles. Balanced development requires attention to scapular control (proper shoulder blade movement and positioning), rotator cuff strength (stabilizing the shoulder joint during overhead actions), and pushing/pulling balance (maintaining appropriate strength ratios between opposing muscle groups).

Balanced strength development directly improves your serving consistency, attack power, and ability to maintain technique during long tournaments.

Strength Development by Age Group
For Ages 10–12
Focus on bodyweight mastery and proper movement patterns:
- bodyweight squats and lunges with perfect form
- modified push-ups and pull-ups
- core stability work (planks, bird dogs)
- medicine ball exercises with light weights (2–4 lbs)
- introduction to resistance bands for external load

For Ages 13–15
Begin progressive external loading with continued technique emphasis:
- goblet squats and split squats

- push-up progressions and assisted pull-ups
- medicine ball rotational exercises (4–6 lbs)
- resistance band complexes for upper body
- introduction to lightweight dumbbells for basic movements

For Ages 16–18

Develop sport-specific strength with appropriate loading:
- barbell squats and deadlifts (with qualified instruction)
- dumbbell and kettlebell complexes
- weighted pull-ups and advanced push-up variations
- plyometric integration (depth jumps, box jumps)
- position-specific strength emphasis

If You Only Do One Thing...

- Prioritize posterior chain development (glutes and hamstrings) for jumping power.
- Focus on scapular strength to protect shoulders during overhead movements.
- Maintain balanced development between pushing and pulling muscles.

Properly developed strength creates the foundation for explosive jumping, powerful attacks, and injury resistance during the physically demanding volleyball season.

AGILITY AND REACTION DEVELOPMENT

Volleyball demands exceptional reactive agility—the ability to quickly and precisely respond to unpredictable stimuli.

This skill combines several physical components including perceptual speed (how quickly you recognize relevant cues), decision-making speed (how rapidly you determine appropriate responses), movement initiation (how effectively you start your movement), change-of-direction efficiency (how smoothly you redirect force), and technique under pressure (how well you maintain mechanics during high-speed situations).

The Progression Model

Agility development follows a clear progression:

1. **Closed-skill linear movement**: Begin with predetermined movements in a single direction: acceleration mechanics, deceleration control, and body positioning.

2. **Closed-skill multi-directional movement**: Advance to predetermined movements in multiple directions: lateral movement efficiency, transitional footwork, and posture maintenance during direction changes.

3. **Open-skill reactive movement**: Progress to unpredictable movements requiring quick reactions: visual stimulus response, auditory cue reaction, and decision-making under time constraints.

4. **Volleyball-specific contextual movement**: Finally, integrate movements into volleyball-specific scenarios: game-situation decision trees, position-specific movement patterns, and fatigue-resistant technique maintenance.

This progressive approach directly enhances your ability to make those game-changing defensive plays and position yourself perfectly for attacking opportunities.

Agility Development by Age Group
For Ages 10–12
Focus on fundamental movement mechanics:
- straight-line sprints with proper starting position
- lane shuffle drills emphasizing low position
- simple cone patterns at moderate speeds
- "Red light/Green light" reaction games
- "mirror" partner drills for basic reactions

For Ages 13–15
Develop multi-directional efficiency:
- T-drill and modified T-drill variations
- ladder drills for foot quickness
- directional change drills with visual cues
- ball drop reaction drills
- defensive shadow drills with coach pointing directions

For Ages 16–18
Integrate volleyball-specific reactive elements:
- multi-directional reaction drills to ball drop
- decision-making drills based on setter movements
- defense-to-attack transition sequences
- multi-ball defensive reaction patterns
- game-simulation movement complexes

Quick Wins for Agility Development

- Practice defensive ready position with weight on balls of feet.
- Focus on first-step quickness in multiple directions.
- Incorporate visual reaction cues in simple drills.

Improved agility directly translates to better court coverage, more effective transition movement between offense and defense, and the ability to make those spectacular plays that energize your entire team.

JUMPING AND LANDING MECHANICS

Volleyball players may perform hundreds of jumps in a single match, making jump quality and landing safety critical priorities.

The Jump Progression

Effective jumping development follows this sequence:

1. **Landing mechanics**: Before focusing on explosive jumping, master absorption mechanics: soft landings with appropriate joint flexion, force distribution through the entire foot, proper alignment of ankles, knees, and hips, and torso position and control.

2. **Countermovement control**: Develop proper loading mechanics, such as coordinated ankle, knee, and hip flexion, upper body positioning, arm swing timing, and rate of force development.

3. **Approach integration**: Connect horizontal momentum with vertical explosion: penultimate step mechanics, approach angle considerations, arm swing coordination, and visual target maintenance.

4. **Volleyball-specific applications**: Apply jumping skills to specific volleyball demands: block jumps (often from static positions), attack jumps (from approach movements), jump serves (with complex coordination demands), and defensive jumps (often from compromised positions).

Proper jumping mechanics directly impact your hitting height, blocking effectiveness, and ability to stay healthy throughout the season.

Jump Development by Age Group
For Ages 10–12
Emphasize landing mechanics and basic jumps:
- "stick the landing" drills, focusing on balance and control
- basic two-foot vertical jumps with proper arm swing
- box jumps onto low, stable surfaces (6–12 inches)
- jumping and landing on lines with a balance focus
- introduction to approach footwork without jumping

For Ages 13–15
Develop countermovement efficiency and basic approaches:
- depth jumps from low heights (12–18 inches)
- three-step approach practice with controlled jumps
- block footwork with submaximal jumps
- consecutive jumps with proper landing mechanics
- medicine ball overhead throws for arm swing coordination

For Ages 16–18

Refine volleyball-specific jumping applications:

- position-specific jumping patterns
- block-to-attack transition jumps
- approach variations (four-step, three-step, emergency two-step)
- single-leg stability and jumping progressions
- maximum height training with proper recovery periods

If You Only Do One Thing...

- Master "quiet" landings to reduce joint stress and improve control.
- Practice arm swing timing to maximize jumping height.
- Focus on the penultimate step (second-to-last) in your approach for power transfer.

Perfecting your jumping mechanics directly increases your hitting reach, improves blocking effectiveness against taller opponents, and protects your knees for volleyball longevity.

VOLLEYBALL-SPECIFIC CONDITIONING

Volleyball's energy system demands unique conditioning approaches. The sport features brief, intense rallies (typically 5-15 seconds) interspersed with short recovery periods (10-20 seconds), repeated over extended match durations.

Energy System Profile

Volleyball primarily challenges two energy systems:

Phosphagen System (ATP-PC)

This is the primary energy source for explosive movements.

- It provides energy for 0–10 seconds of maximal effort.
- It is crucial for jumps, sprints, and explosive skills.
- It requires 3–5 minutes for complete recovery.

Glycolytic System (Anaerobic)

This is the secondary energy source for extended rallies.

- It provides energy for 10–60 seconds of high-intensity effort.
- It supports repeated explosive efforts with incomplete recovery.
- It generates lactate as a byproduct.

Understanding these energy systems helps you train specifically for volleyball's unique demands rather than wasting time on lengthy cardio that doesn't transfer to the court.

Conditioning Methods by Age Group

For Ages 10–12

Focus on fun, game-based conditioning:

- volleyball-specific tag games
- short sprint relays (under 10 seconds)
- modified small-court games (1v1, 2v2)
- jump rope intervals (20 seconds work, 40 seconds rest)
- "Beat the ball" movement challenges

For Ages 13–15

Develop alactic power and beginning capacity:

- 5–8 second sprint or bound sequences
- 30–45 second recovery periods
- small-sided games with continuous play (30–45 seconds)
- line touch progressions with direction changes
- position-specific movement patterns

For Ages 16–18

Train both alactic and glycolytic systems with volleyball specificity:

- 6-second maximum effort drills with 45-second recovery
- position-specific movement sequences
- 30-second high-intensity efforts with 60-second recovery
- game-simulation conditioning with tactical elements
- tournament-style conditioning (multiple short sessions with incomplete recovery)

Quick Wins for Volleyball Conditioning

- Focus on short, intense efforts rather than long, continuous training.
- Use small-court games for sport-specific conditioning.
- Train recovery capacity between explosive efforts.

Sport-specific conditioning directly impacts your performance in long matches and tournaments, allowing you to maintain jumping height and movement quality during critical late-game points.

NUTRITION AND HYDRATION FOR YOUNG VOLLEYBALL ATHLETES

Proper nutrition powers optimal performance and supports long-term development. Young volleyball players have unique nutritional needs due to growth and development requirements, high energy expenditure from training and competition, frequent tournament play with multiple matches in short timeframes, and often-challenging eating schedules around school and practices.

Age-Specific Nutrition Guidelines
For Ages 10–12

Focus on establishing healthy habits:

- regular meal and snack schedule
- hydration emphasis with water as the primary beverage
- a variety of whole foods from all food groups
- pre-activity snacks (fruit, yogurt, granola)
- post-activity recovery with chocolate milk or similar
- parent education on proper fueling for young athletes

For Ages 13–15

Develop nutritional awareness with increased training demands:

- increased caloric needs during growth spurts
- protein distribution throughout the day
- tournament day nutrition planning
- hydration monitoring strategies
- understanding of pre-/during-/post-exercise nutrition timing
- introduction to sports nutrition concepts

For Ages 16–18

Implement performance nutrition strategies:

- individualized nutrition approaches
- strategic fueling for training and competition
- recovery nutrition protocols
- hydration and electrolyte management
- body composition considerations with health emphasis
- advanced tournament nutrition planning

Proper nutrition directly impacts your energy levels during long tournament days, your recovery between matches, and your overall development as an athlete.

Tournament Nutrition Strategies

Volleyball tournaments present unique challenges with multiple matches over extended periods. Strategic approaches include the following:

Pre-Tournament Preparation

- carbohydrate focus for 24–48 hours before competition
- increased fluid intake leading into tournament day
- well-balanced dinner the night before
- adequate sleep to support recovery processes

Tournament Day Planning

- familiar, easily-digestible breakfast 2–3 hours before play
- cooler packed with appropriate options for the entire day
- hydration supplies (water bottle plus electrolyte supplements)

- mental plan for eating between matches despite potential nervousness

Between-Match Nutrition

- rapidly absorbing carbohydrates immediately after matches
- small protein amounts (10–15 g) for recovery support
- hydration emphasis, including electrolyte replacement
- easily digestible options that won't cause gastrointestinal distress

If You Only Do One Thing...

- Never begin a match dehydrated—monitor urine color for a light straw shade.
- Plan tournament nutrition the day before rather than improvising.
- Always consume something within 30 minutes after activity.

Strategic tournament nutrition directly impacts your performance in late-day matches when many players falter due to inadequate fueling and hydration.

RECOVERY METHODS FOR GROWING BODIES

Young athletes need more recovery time than adult athletes. Their bodies simultaneously manage volleyball training and competition demands, academic and social stress, growth and development processes, and neurological system maturation.

Recovery Implementation by Age Group
For Ages 10–12

Focus on fundamental recovery habits:

- sleep education and prioritization (9–10 hours nightly)
- basic static stretching routine after activity
- proper cool-down activities after practice
- consistent hydration habits
- enjoyable activities outside of volleyball

For Ages 13–15

Develop consistent recovery routines:

- sleep quality monitoring and improvement
- dynamic flexibility routines
- basic foam rolling introduction
- recovery nutrition implementation
- stress management techniques
- active recovery activities on off days

For Ages 16–18

Implement comprehensive recovery systems:

- individualized flexibility protocols
- advanced soft tissue work
- contrast therapy, when available (hot/cold)
- planned recovery days in training
- recovery metrics tracking
- strategic recovery during tournament weekends

Quick Wins for Recovery
- Prioritize sleep above all other recovery methods.
- Develop a 10-minute post-practice flexibility routine.
- Consume protein and carbohydrates within 30 minutes after training.

Proper recovery directly affects your ability to train consistently, reduce injury risk, and maintain performance quality throughout the competitive season.

PUTTING IT ALL TOGETHER: THE VOLLEYBALL ATHLETE DEVELOPMENT SYSTEM

Athletic development for volleyball requires a systematic, progressive approach that respects biological development while building sport-specific qualities.

Weekly Physical Development Template Example
For Ages 10–12
- **Monday:** movement skills and volleyball practice
- **Tuesday:** basic strength development and flexibility
- **Wednesday:** volleyball practice with coordination emphasis
- **Thursday:** active recovery day with light movement
- **Friday:** volleyball practice with game focus
- **Weekend:** competition or structured free play

For Ages 13–15
- **Monday:** strength training and volleyball practice
- **Tuesday:** movement skill development and conditioning

- **Wednesday:** volleyball practice with recovery emphasis
- **Thursday:** strength training (upper body focus) and agility
- **Friday:** pre-competition preparation and skills
- **Weekend:** competition with recovery protocols

For Ages 16–18

- **Monday:** strength training (lower body) and volleyball practice
- **Tuesday:** power development and technical skills
- **Wednesday:** recovery day with mobility and low-intensity skills
- **Thursday:** strength training (upper body) and volleyball practice
- **Friday:** pre-competition preparation
- **Weekend:** competition with strategic recovery

If You Only Do One Thing...

- Implement a consistent weekly structure that balances training stress and recovery.
- Include at least one dedicated recovery day each week.
- Track your progress with simple performance metrics (vertical jump, agility times).

A systematic approach to physical development directly enhances your volleyball performance while reducing injury risk and supporting long-term athletic development.

FINAL THOUGHTS: THE PHYSICAL JOURNEY

Physical development for volleyball represents a continuous process rather than a destination. The most successful athletes view physical preparation as an ongoing practice rather than a finite accomplishment.

Remember these guiding principles as you develop your volleyball body:

- **Consistency trumps intensity**: Regular, moderate training produces better long-term results than sporadic, extreme efforts.

- **Movement quality precedes movement quantity**: How you move matters more than how much you move.

- **Recovery enables adaptation**: The improvement process occurs during recovery, not during training itself.

- **Patience yields resilience**: Gradual progression builds sustainable athletic development with fewer setbacks.

- **Athletic identity transcends volleyball**: The physical qualities you develop through volleyball will serve you throughout your lifetime.

The volleyball court rewards the prepared body. By respecting the physical development process and implementing these principles consistently, you'll build the athletic foundation that allows your volleyball skills to flourish.

The next chapter awaits, where we'll explore the fundamental technical skill of passing—the foundation upon which all volleyball excellence builds.

CHAPTER 3:
MASTER THE FUNDAMENTALS—
PASSING AND BALL CONTROL

When a powerful spike thunders across the net at 50 mph, what stands between your team and instant defeat? A well-executed pass.

Passing may not capture the glory of a spectacular attack, but make no mistake: it forms the absolute foundation upon which all volleyball success is built. The quality of your first contact directly determines your team's offensive capabilities. As the volleyball adage goes, "Without a pass, there is no attack."

PASSING SKILL PROGRESSION CHECKLIST

Foundation Skills

- ☐ Maintain a flat platform during contact.
- ☐ Position body behind the ball with shoulders square to target.

☐ Generate power from legs rather than swinging arms.

☐ Control ball direction with platform angle, not arm swing.

Movement Skills

☐ Move efficiently to position body behind the ball.

☐ Maintain low center of gravity throughout movement.

☐ Square shoulders to target before contact.

☐ Move backward while maintaining sight of the ball.

Ball Control Skills

☐ Adjust to different serve types (float vs. topspin).

☐ Control ball trajectory for consistent setter distance.

☐ Pass shorter/deeper based on situation.

☐ Redirect hard-driven balls with control.

Mental and Communication Skills

☐ Call the ball early and loudly.

☐ Maintain consistent pre-pass routine.

☐ Recover quickly from errors.

☐ Recognize and respond to server tendencies.

THE FOUNDATION: PROPER READY POSITION

Before contact ever occurs, successful passing begins with a strong, balanced, ready position. This athletic stance creates the foundation for all defensive movements and prepares your body to respond to incoming serves or attacks.

The "platform" refers to the flat surface created by extending and joining your forearms. This platform redirects the ball rather than attempting to "catch" or "push" it—a critical distinction for newer players to understand.

For an effective ready position:

- feet slightly wider than shoulder-width apart
- weight balanced on the balls of your feet
- knees bent to lower center of gravity
- right foot slightly forward if right-handed (reverse for lefties)
- torso leaning slightly forward from the hips with flat back
- shoulders forward of knees, head up, eyes on server/ attacker
- arms extended forward with slight elbow bend
- wrists pronated (turned inward) with thumbs parallel and downward

For Ages 10–12: Focus on establishing a basic athletic position with bent knees, extended arms, and a flat platform, keeping eyes on the server and weight forward on the balls of your feet.

For Ages 13–15: Refine this position with balanced weight distribution, consistent platform angle, pre-contact adjustments based on server position, lower center of gravity, and "loaded" legs ready for quick movement.

For Ages 16–18: Incorporate position adjustments based on scouting information, subtle weight shifts anticipating serve direction, pre-contact communication with teammates, and position variations based on defensive systems.

A well-executed ready position allows you to react quickly to unexpected serves, giving your team a significantly better chance of running a planned offensive play rather than scrambling after a poor first contact.

Quick Wins for Ready Position

- Keep weight on the balls of your feet, never flat-footed.
- Create a flat forearm platform with wrists pronated.
- Position with your knees bent and torso leaning slightly forward.
- Keep your head up with eyes focused on the server.
- Mentally prepare for movement in any direction.

THE FOREARM PASS: BUILDING YOUR FOUNDATION

The forearm pass forms the cornerstone of volleyball ball control. When performed correctly, this technique allows players to accurately direct balls that are too low for overhead setting and provides stability for handling powerful serves and attacks.

Key technical elements:

- ball contact on flat forearm surface, 2–4 inches above wrists
- avoid contact on hands or wrists
- arms create single flat, angled surface
- contact occurs in front of body, not under face
- legs drive the passing action, not arms
- shoulders square to target
- platform angle directed toward target
- hands together with firm wrists
- platform moves as a unit without swinging arms

- power from legs pushing through floor
- control through platform angle, not pushing

Mastering the forearm pass directly increases your team's offensive options by giving your setter consistent, predictable passes that allow them to set all hitting positions.

Common Errors and Corrections

For Ages 10–12

- **Error:** swinging arms up at the ball
- **Correction:** Practice "freeze" passes, holding platform position after contact.
- **Error:** ball contacting hands instead of forearms
- **Correction:** Use visual markers like sweatbands to identify proper contact point.
- **Error:** platform breaking apart at contact
- **Correction:** Experiment with different hand-grip techniques to find secure position.

For Ages 13–15

- **Error:** ball passing too low over the net
- **Correction:** Focus on platform angle—slightly more upward for deeper passes.
- **Error:** inconsistent passing accuracy
- **Correction:** Ensure body is behind ball with shoulders square to target.
- **Error:** late or inappropriate footwork
- **Correction:** Emphasize "ball-body-target" movement sequence.

For Ages 16–18

- **Error:** difficulty controlling spin or pace
- **Correction:** Develop "give" in platform by adjusting extension based on ball speed.
- **Error:** struggle with short/deep adjustment
- **Correction:** Practice early recognition of ball trajectory.
- **Error:** inconsistency under pressure
- **Correction:** Incorporate decision-making elements into passing drills.

Eliminating these common passing errors helps your team maintain system play, which can increase attack efficiency by over 20% compared to out-of-system situations.

If You Only Do One Thing…

- Focus on controlling the ball with platform angle rather than swinging at the ball.
- Position your body behind the ball with your shoulders facing the target.
- Keep your platform stable through contact without breaking at the wrists.
- Use your legs to generate power rather than swinging your arms.
- Watch the ball all the way to your platform.

MOVEMENT TO THE BALL: POSITIONING FOR SUCCESS

Great passing begins before the ball crosses the net. Your ability to read, move, and position yourself determines passing success more than the actual contact itself.

Reading server cues:

- Server position indicates potential serve direction.
- Toss height and location reveal serving style and trajectory.
- Shoulder and hip alignment indicates the intended direction.
- Contact point shows serve speed and direction.
- Ball rotation reveals float serve vs. topspin serve.

Movement Development by Age Group
For Ages 10–12
Focus on basic movement fundamentals:

- shuffle steps for short distances
- crossover steps for medium distances
- run-stop-pass sequence for longer distances
- moving to place ball between shoulders

For Ages 13–15
Develop more efficient movement:

- proper approach angles to maintain ball vision
- transitions from large to small adjustment steps
- improved cross-step technique for lateral movement
- balanced stopping positions before contact

For Ages 16–18
Refine advanced movement:

- recognition-based movement patterns
- serve-specific defensive positioning

- quick directional changes while maintaining balance
- recovery movements after passing

Footwork Direction Guidelines

Forward Movement

- Begin with small drop step in direction of ball.
- Lead with foot closest to ball's direction.
- Keep shoulders square to target.
- Decelerate with short, controlled steps.
- Establish stable base before contact.

Lateral Movement

- Start with step in direction of movement.
- Shuffle for short distances (feet don't cross).
- Use crossover steps for longer distances.
- Maintain low center of gravity.
- Square shoulders to target before contact.

Backward Movement

- Begin with drop step backward.
- Keep eyes on ball (fight tendency to turn).
- Slight forward lean to counterbalance backward movement.

Teams with efficient movement skills maintain significantly higher serve-receive averages, translating to more points scored from planned offensive plays rather than out-of-system scrambles.

Quick Wins for Movement to the Ball

- Keep your first movement step small to maintain balance.
- Stay low throughout your movement rather than standing up while moving.
- Square your shoulders to target before contact, not during or after.
- Practice backward movement specifically—it's the most challenging direction.
- Watch the server's contact point rather than just the ball flight.

PASSING PROGRESSION AND SKILL DEVELOPMENT

Passing skills develop progressively through four key stages:

1. **Stationary Control (Form Focus)**
   - partner tosses with predictable trajectory
   - self-toss pass to self
   - wall passing with controlled rebounds
   - focus on platform presentation and consistent contact point

2. **Movement Integration (Position Focus)**
   - short movement patterns before passing
   - predictable tosses requiring single direction movement
   - focus on footwork patterns and stopping balance
   - emphasis on body position behind ball

3. **Variable Trajectory (Adaptation Focus)**
   - mixed high/low/short/deep tosses
   - varied speeds and trajectories

o   spin variation (float vs. topspin)

o   focus on reading ball flight early

o   platform adjustments for different balls

4. **Game Simulation (Pressure Focus)**

o   live serving in game-like positions

o   competitive scoring elements

o   decision-making components

o   communication with teammates

o   consistency under pressure

Moving methodically through this progression develops passing consistency under pressure, which directly correlates with offensive efficiency and match success rates.

Recommended Drills by Age Group
For Ages 10–12

- **Partner pass freeze:** Partner tosses ball; passer creates platform and contacts ball; passer "freezes" position after contact for 2 seconds.
- **Triangle passing:** Three players form triangle 12 feet apart; ball passed clockwise then counterclockwise.
- **Wall control series:** Pass ball against wall repeatedly; focus on consistent rebounding height.

For Ages 13–15

- **Pass and move:** After passing, player moves laterally one step; partner passes to new position.
- **Three-zone passing:** Court divided into three zones; passer must move to indicated zone and pass to target.

- **Pass-set-pass drill:** Passer starts in position 5; passes to position 2; target sets back; original passer makes second pass to position 3.

For Ages 16–18

- **Serve-pass-hit sequence:** Game-like formation; server aims at specific passers; setter delivers to designated hitter.
- **Scramble pass:** Passer starts centered; runs to touch sideline; must return to pass ball.
- **Defensive transition passing:** Dig ball to target; transition to serve receive positions; pass immediate serve.

If You Only Do One Thing...

- Incorporate some form of passing practice into every training session.
- Begin each passing session with controlled, technique-focused repetitions.
- Gradually increase difficulty by adding movement before contact.
- Always include game-like serving patterns in your passing practice.
- Create competitive elements that reward passing accuracy.

DEVELOPING TOUCH AND BALL CONTROL

Beyond basic technique lies the art of "touch," the ability to control pace, spin, and trajectory with subtle adjustments. This skill separates good passers from exceptional ones.

Platform Angle Control

Subtle adjustments guide the ball's path:

- upward angle = deeper passes
- flatter angle = shorter passes
- left/right angling = lateral direction adjustment

Contact Point Adjustments

Influence trajectory:

- higher contact point (closer to elbows) = steeper path
- lower contact point (closer to wrists) = flatter trajectory
- centered contact = direct passes
- slight off-center contact = directional adjustments

Body "Give"

Affects pace management:

- slight knee flex upon contact absorbs pace from hard-driven balls
- less "give" adds energy to slower balls
- platform remains stable while legs provide cushioning

Touch Development by Age Group

- **For Ages 10–12:** Focus on basic control and consistency through target passing, high-low alternating wall passes, and partner distance variations.
- **For Ages 13–15:** Develop finer control with accuracy zones, pace variation exercises, and trajectory control drills.

- **For Ages 16–18:** Refine advanced touch with one-arm control practice, platform angle series, setter-distance passing, and velocity control exercises.

Superior ball control enables passers to deliver consistent targets to setters even from challenging serves, increasing offensive conversion rates by 15–20% compared to teams with inconsistent first contacts.

Quick Wins for Ball Control Development

- Focus on a consistent contact point on your platform for predictable results.
- Control ball direction primarily through platform angle, not arm swing.
- Practice passing to specific targets rather than just "up and in front."
- Develop the ability to control both fast and slow serves with the same technique.
- Learn to "absorb" hard-driven balls with slight knee flex at contact.

OVERHEAD PASSING TECHNIQUE

While the forearm pass forms the foundation of ball control, the overhead pass provides an important alternative for higher balls. This technique allows for greater accuracy on higher-trajectory serves and free balls.

The overhead pass becomes appropriate when:

- ball trajectory is above shoulder height
- you have time to position directly beneath the ball
- incoming ball has manageable pace

- rules allow it (standards vary by competition level)
- maximum accuracy is needed on first contact

For Ages 13–15: Focus on basic hand position similar to setting, positioning directly under the ball, contacting with fingerpads rather than palms, and making clear, clean contact without prolonged holding.

For Ages 16–18: Develop quick transitions between ready position and overhead position, sound judgment regarding when to use overhead versus forearm technique, and understanding of referee interpretations at different levels.

Note: This skill is generally not emphasized for players under 13, who should first focus on developing strong forearm passing fundamentals.

Teams that effectively integrate overhead passing into their defensive system create more offensive flexibility, allowing setters to deliver consistent sets to all hitting positions, even after challenging serves.

Quick Wins for Overhead Passing
- Position your body directly under the ball before contact.
- Create a solid hand position with fingers spread and relaxed.
- Make contact with fingerpads, not palms, for better control.
- Keep contact brief but controlled to avoid violations.
- Practice transitioning between forearm and overhead techniques.

MENTAL APPROACH TO PASSING

The psychological aspect of passing often determines success more than physical technique. A strong mental approach creates consistency under pressure and helps recover quickly from inevitable errors.

Serving Reception Focus

- Begin focus before server contacts ball.
- Commit to movement toward ball.
- Take responsibility for "your area" plus seam help.
- Communicate clearly and early.
- Maintain confidence despite errors.

Defensive Passing Mindset

- Read-react sequence starting with attacker cues.
- Commit to platform control on hard-driven balls.
- Willingness to sacrifice body position when necessary.
- Focus on recovery after each contact.
- Persistent effort on every defensive opportunity.

Mental Skills by Age Group

- **For Ages 10–12:** Focus on effort over outcome, process praise for proper technique, simple pre-pass routine, and positive self-talk after errors.
- **For Ages 13–15:** Build error management techniques, consistent pre-pass routines, specific focus cues, and simple error recovery strategies.

- **For Ages 16–18:** Implement pressure training with game simulation, detailed visualization, distraction training, and performance under fatigue training.

Communication Development by Age Group
- **For Ages 10–12:** Master basic calls like "Mine" or "Ball," "Help," and "Short" or "Deep" with sufficient volume and consistent terminology.
- **For Ages 13–15:** Add "Mine-mine" for emphasis, direction calls, serve type identification, earlier call timing, and non-verbal communication.
- **For Ages 16–18:** Establish clear seam responsibilities, implement play calls after reception, integrate blocker communication, and share server tendency information.

Players with consistent mental routines demonstrate up to 25% better passing performance under pressure than those without established mental preparation processes.

If You Only Do One Thing...
- Develop a consistent pre-pass routine to focus your concentration.
- Call the ball early and loudly to avoid teammate confusion.
- Reset mentally after each play, regardless of the previous outcome.
- Focus on the server's contact point rather than the ball trajectory.

- Practice passing under pressure to build situational confidence.

PASSING IN DIFFERENT SYSTEMS

As players advance, passing becomes integrated into broader team systems. Understanding these systems helps passers fulfill their role within the team structure.

Common Serve Reception Formations

Two-Person Serve Receive

- primarily used in beach volleyball
- each passer responsible for half the court
- greater court coverage requirement per player
- emphasis on communication at middle seam

Three-Person Serve Receive

- most common youth formation
- primary pattern for 6-6, 4-2, and 6-2 offenses
- balanced court coverage responsibility
- priority communication on two seams

Four-Person Serve Receive

- used against strong jump servers
- provides maximum court coverage
- often used in 5-1 offensive systems
- reduced individual court responsibility

Five-Person Serve Receive

- used against extremely challenging servers
- minimal individual court responsibility
- multiple communication seams to manage

System Integration by Age Group

- **For Ages 13–15:** Learn basic positional roles - outside hitters as primary passers, liberos as passing leaders, middle blockers often removed from primary passing, setters protected in serve receive.
- **For Ages 16–18:** Develop deeper understanding of rotation-specific assignments, situational adjustments, server-specific adaptations, and integration with broader team strategy.

Note: Younger players (under 13) typically focus on basic passing techniques rather than complex systems.

Clear system understanding helps teams maintain significantly higher passing averages, which directly correlates with offensive success and scoring efficiency.

Quick Wins for System Integration

- Know your specific court coverage area in each rotation.
- Understand your passing priority relative to teammates.
- Communicate seam responsibilities before each serve.
- Study and recognize opponent serving patterns.
- Practice movement between serve reception and offensive positions.

BEYOND BASIC PASSING: ADVANCED CONCEPTS

As players develop, additional concepts enhance performance and prepare for higher levels of competition:

Reading Serve Tendencies

- Identify servers' preferred zones and targets.
- Recognize the relationship between server position and direction.
- Observe toss variations indicating serve type.
- Note situational serving tendencies.

Passing Different Serve Types

Jump Serves

- earlier ready position due to increased ball speed
- slightly deeper initial position
- platform angle control for pace management
- increased communication

Jump Float Serves

- awareness of unpredictable ball movement
- "quiet" platform with minimal movement
- extended focus through contact
- preparation for sudden directional changes

Short Serves

- forward-focused ready position
- quick first-step reaction

- modified platform for shorter distance
- clear communication for boundary balls

For Ages 15–16: Begin studying opponent serving patterns, developing specialized techniques for different serve types, and learning to communicate server tendencies.

For Ages 17–18: Implement comprehensive scouting of opponents, develop nuanced platform adjustments, utilize statistical analysis, and integrate passing strategy with team defensive systems.

Teams that effectively scout and adapt to opponent serving tendencies can neutralize even the strongest servers, maintaining offensive efficiency when other teams would struggle.

If You Only Do One Thing...

- Study opponent serving patterns during warm-ups and early game play.
- Make subtle adjustments to your platform based on serve type.
- Track your passing statistics to identify improvement areas.
- Develop specific techniques for jump serves, float serves, and short serves.
- Communicate server tendencies with teammates.

FROM PRACTICE TO PERFORMANCE: THE PASSING JOURNEY

Passing mastery comes through thousands of repetitions and constant refinement. Remember these principles:

- **Consistency over perfection:** Aim for reliable, predictable passing results rather than occasional perfect passes mixed with errors.
- **Process focus over outcome:** Concentrate on proper technique, reading, and movement rather than solely the result.
- **Deliberate practice:** Approach passing work with specific aspects to improve rather than mindless repetition.
- **Pressure progression:** Gradually introduce game-like pressure to build competitive resilience.
- **Technical foundation first:** Build sound mechanical technique before tackling complex game situations.

Consistent, high-quality passing is the single most reliable predictor of team success at all levels of volleyball. Teams with passing averages above 2.2 (on a 3-point scale) win matches at nearly double the rate of teams with passing averages below 2.0.

The path to passing excellence begins with a solid platform, develops through deliberate practice, and culminates in consistent performance under pressure. Every great setter, attacker, and team begins with a great pass—making you, the passer, the true foundation of volleyball excellence.

In the next chapter, we'll explore the art of setting—turning your well-placed pass into the perfect attacking opportunity for your teammates.

CHAPTER 4:

SETTING: THE ART OF DELIVERY

Like a maestro conducting an orchestra or a chess grandmaster anticipating moves in advance, the setter orchestrates every offensive play on the volleyball court. While hitters may deliver the spectacular kills that bring crowds to their feet, it's the setter's hands that create those opportunities, transforming even challenged passes into scoring chances through precision and creativity.

This chapter explores the intricate art of setting—the crucial link that turns defensive efforts into offensive opportunities. Whether you're a dedicated setter or a player developing all-around skills, mastering this position will elevate both your individual performance and your team's offensive potential.

SETTING SKILL PROGRESSION LADDER

1. **Standing sets:** proper hand position and footwork; basic front and back sets

2. **Moving sets:** setting while in motion; transitional footwork

3. **Jump setting:** added height and attack potential; increased offensive speed

4. **Tempo control:** varied speeds and trajectories; consistent location with changing tempos

5. **Deceptive setting:** disguising intent and location; strategic setting against blockers

6. **Advanced system setting:** specialized sets for complex offenses; emergency techniques and adaptations

SETTING SKILL PROGRESSION CHECKLIST

Foundation Skills

☐ Establish proper hand position (triangle/window above forehead).

☐ Contact ball with fingerpads, not palms.

☐ Push through legs, torso, and arms in sequence.

☐ Control ball trajectory with hand positioning and follow-through.

☐ Deliver consistent location to target area.

Movement Skills

☐ Move efficiently to position under the ball.

☐ Square body to target before setting.

☐ Transition quickly from defensive to setting position.

☐ Establish balanced platform before delivery.

☐ Set effectively from various court positions.

Ball Control Skills

- ☐ Adjust to different pass heights and locations.
- ☐ Control set height, speed, and arc.
- ☐ Deliver different tempos appropriate to hitters.
- ☐ Disguise intended set location.
- ☐ Maintain consistency under pressure.

Mental and Communication Skills

- ☐ Develop consistent pre-set routine.
- ☐ Communicate clearly with hitters.
- ☐ Read and respond to defensive alignments.
- ☐ Make quick, decisive set choices.
- ☐ Maintain composure after errors.

THE FOUNDATION: HAND POSITIONING AND BODY MECHANICS

Great setting begins with proper hand position and body alignment. The precision of a set depends largely on the consistency of your hand formation and the mechanics of ball delivery.

Hand Position and Ball Contact

Form a triangular window directly above your forehead by bringing your hands up with thumbs and index fingers, creating a triangle through which you can see the approaching ball. Your fingers should be spread comfortably with a natural curve, not rigid and straight, but not excessively flexed either.

The ball should contact primarily your fingerpads, not your palms or fingertips. Contact with the palms creates a "deep catch" that leads to illegal handling calls, while contact too far on the fingertips provides insufficient control. At contact, your hands should be approximately 3–4 inches apart, positioned above your forehead with elbows comfortably out to the sides at roughly 90-degree angles.

- **For Ages 10–12:** Focus on creating a consistent triangle shape with thumbs and index fingers, positioning hands above the forehead (not in front of the face), and contacting the ball with fingerpads rather than palms.

- **For Ages 13–15:** Refine hand position with attention to finger spacing, consistent contact points across all fingers, and appropriate tension in the hands—firm enough for control but relaxed enough for feel.

- **For Ages 16–18:** Develop advanced hand position awareness, including subtle adjustments for different set types, ability to maintain proper position during jump setting, and proprioceptive feel for the ball.

Consistent hand positioning directly impacts set accuracy, with proper technique resulting in up to 30% more precise sets compared to inconsistent hand formation.

Body Position and Movement Sequence

Setting is a full-body skill that begins with the legs and finishes with the fingertips. The power sequence flows from the ground up through a coordinated chain:

1. **Base position:** Begin with feet shoulder-width apart, knees slightly bent, weight balanced on balls of feet.

2. **Loading phase:** As the ball approaches, bend knees further to create power potential.

3. **Extension sequence:** Delivery begins with leg drive through the floor, transfers through the torso, continues through the arms, and finishes with controlled wrist and finger action.

4. **Follow-through:** After contact, continue the extension pattern with hands following toward the target.

The entire motion should be smooth and coordinated rather than segmented. Think of it as similar to shooting a basketball—power from the legs, guidance from the hands, with all body segments working in harmony.

Proper body mechanics enable setters to maintain consistency throughout long matches, when fatigue often causes technique breakdown for less disciplined players.

Quick Wins for Setting Fundamentals

- Position hands in a triangle shape directly above the forehead, not in front of the face.
- Contact the ball with fingerpads, not palms or fingertips.
- Generate power from legs first, then arms, then fingers.
- Keep eyes focused on the ball through a consistent contact point.
- Follow through with hands toward the target direction.

SETTING FOOTWORK AND MOVEMENT PATTERNS

Unlike passing or attacking, setting requires you to position your body directly beneath the ball with your shoulders square to your target. This precise positioning demands specific movement patterns.

Movement to the Ball

Efficient setter footwork follows these principles:

1. **Read early:** Begin reading the pass trajectory immediately, identifying where the ball will land.

2. **Quick first step:** Initiate movement with a decisive drop step in the direction of the ball.

3. **Direct path:** Move in as straight a line as possible to the setting position—avoid circular or arcing pathways.

4. **Deceleration control:** As you approach the setting position, transition from larger to smaller steps, establishing balance.

5. **Squared stance:** Complete your movement with shoulders square to the intended target and balanced weight distribution.

The specific footwork pattern depends on the distance:

- **Short distances:** Use shuffle steps that maintain an athletic stance.
- **Medium distances:** Utilize a cross-step pattern.
- **Longer distances:** Employ a run-stop-set sequence.

For Ages 10–12: Focus on basic movement with emphasis on getting the body under the ball before setting. Establish the concept of "run to the spot, then set" rather than attempting to set while still moving.

For Ages 13–15: Develop more refined footwork with specific cross-step patterns and better deceleration control. Work on square positioning relative to different attack zones.

For Ages 16–18: Master advanced movement techniques including efficient footwork from defensive positions, quick transitions for second-contact attacks, and subtle pre-set adjustments based on offensive strategy.

Efficient setter movement directly influences offensive tempo, with elite setters able to establish position approximately 0.2 seconds faster than intermediate setters—a difference that dramatically impacts the effectiveness of quick attacks.

Great setters also maintain constant awareness of court position without looking away from the ball. This "spatial awareness" develops through deliberate practice and understanding of court landmarks like antennas, attack line, sidelines, and net position.

Quick Wins for Setting Movement

- Read the pass trajectory early to begin movement immediately.
- Move directly to the target position rather than in arcs or curves.
- Transition from speed to control with decelerating footwork.
- Establish shoulders square to the intended target.
- Develop peripheral vision awareness of court landmarks.

SET TYPES AND BALL CONTROL

A versatile setter delivers various set types that create diverse attacking options. Understanding the characteristics and applications of different sets adds essential tools to your setting repertoire.

Set Height Classifications

- **High sets (3–4):** slow-tempo sets with significant height and hang time
- **Medium sets (2–2.5):** moderate height with medium tempo
- **Quick sets (1–1.5):** fast tempo with minimal height
- **Shoots/Gos (0.5):** ultra-quick sets with almost no vertical height

Set Distance Classifications

- **Tight:** very close to the net (risk of net violations, but difficult to block)
- **Off:** approximately 3–5 feet off the net (optimal for most attacks)
- **Far:** further from the net (safer but limits attack angles)

Set Location Classifications

- **Outside/Left (Position 4):** sets to the left antenna area
- **Middle (Position 3):** sets to the center of the net

- **Right/Opposite (Position 2):** sets to the right antenna area
- **Pipe/D (Position 6):** sets to back-row attackers in center back

For Ages 10–12: Focus primarily on high, looping sets to the outside (left) and right positions. Emphasize consistent location about 3–4 feet off the net rather than tight sets.

For Ages 13–15: Develop medium-height sets and begin incorporating back-sets to position 2. Introduce basic quick sets to the middle position and begin working on set consistency at different distances from the net.

For Ages 16–18: Master the full range of set tempos, including quick/shoots, advanced combination plays, and sets from various court positions. Develop precise distance control for tight versus off sets.

A setter's ability to deliver multiple set tempos creates significant offensive advantages, with multi-tempo offenses typically scoring 25–30% more points than single-tempo strategies.

Setting Trajectory Control

Controlling set trajectory requires mastery of these technical elements:

1. **Release point:** Where the ball leaves your hands determines much of the set's trajectory. Higher release points generally create flatter, faster sets.

2. **Hand position at contact:** The angle of your hands at contact significantly impacts set direction. For front sets, hands should generally face upward and slightly

forward. For back sets, the hand position adjusts to face more upward and slightly backward.

3. **Wrist flexibility:** Wrist action provides fine control over the set's final trajectory. Firmer wrists generally create more direct, fast sets, while slightly softer wrists allow for more touch and control.

4. **Follow-through direction:** The follow-through dramatically influences set accuracy. Your hands should continue in the intended direction of the set, reaching toward the target.

Precise trajectory control enables setters to create optimal hitting approaches, with properly located sets increasing hitting efficiency by as much as 40% compared to sets that force hitters to adjust.

Quick Wins for Set Types and Control
- Develop distinct height differences between set types.
- Control set trajectory with hand angle at release.
- Focus on a consistent set distance from the net.
- Practice the direct relationship between follow-through and accuracy.
- Learn to modify trajectory based on pass quality.

SETTING DECISION-MAKING AND STRATEGY

Beyond technical execution, setting excellence depends on strategic decision-making that creates advantageous attack scenarios. Great setters are tactical masterminds who manipulate opposing blockers and maximize their hitters' strengths.

Reading the Defense

Effective setters constantly gather and process defensive information:

- **Blocker positioning:** Note pre-play alignment of opposition blockers, identifying which zones might have slower blocker movements.
- **Middle blocker reading:** Track the opposing middle blocker's commitment and tendencies, looking for opportunities to set away from their strength.
- **Defensive coverage patterns:** Identify gaps in the defensive coverage based on their base formation.

For Ages 10–12: Introduce basic defensive awareness, primarily focusing on the concept of "setting away from multiple blockers." Keep decision-making simple.

For Ages 13–15: Develop more nuanced blocker reading, particularly tracking the opposing middle blocker. Introduce the concept of setting the "hot hitter."

For Ages 16–18: Master advanced defensive reading, including blocker tendencies, recognition of defensive systems, and adaptation to the opposing team's strategic adjustments.

Strategic setting decisions that account for defensive alignments can increase team hitting efficiency by 15–25%, with the most significant gains occurring against strong blocking teams.

Setter's Communication Checklist
Pre-Play Communication

- call offensive play/set plan

- alert hitters to blocker tendencies
- confirm coverage responsibilities

During-Play Communication
- call for the ball ("Mine!")
- tempo cue to hitters
- transition direction for teammates

After-Set Communication
- transition cue for next action
- coverage position call
- attack encouragement

Between-Points Communication
- strategic adjustments
- positive reinforcement
- next-play focus

Effective setters use clear, consistent communication that directs teammates, builds confidence, and implements strategy. Your communication system should develop with age and experience:

- **For Ages 10–12:** Develop basic communication habits including simple pre-play signals and consistent, clear calls ("Mine," "Help," etc.).
- **For Ages 13–15:** Establish more detailed communication, including specific play calls, blocker movement information, and supportive feedback techniques.

- **For Ages 16–18:** Master comprehensive communication systems, including tactical information, subtle non-verbal cues, and leadership techniques that motivate different personality types.

Great setter communication can reduce team errors by up to 30% while significantly increasing offensive efficiency through improved coordination and confidence.

Quick Wins for Setting Strategy

- Track the opposing middle blocker's movement patterns.
- Develop awareness of each hitter's strengths and preferences.
- Establish consistent locations before introducing variations.
- Use simple hand signals to communicate play decisions.
- Consider the score and situation when selecting a set location.

ADVANCED SETTING TECHNIQUES

As setters develop, they add sophisticated techniques that expand offensive possibilities and create greater defensive uncertainty.

Jump Setting

Jump setting adds offense versatility through multiple advantages:

- **Contact height:** Setting from a higher point creates different attack angles and potentially quicker deliveries.
- **Attack threat:** The setter becomes an offensive threat, forcing middle blockers to respect their attack potential.

- **Deception enhancement:** The identical approach for both setting and attacking creates greater deception.
- **Timing advantages:** Jump setting potentially delivers the ball more quickly to attackers, creating blocking challenges.

For Ages 10–12: Focus on standing setting fundamentals before introducing jump setting.

For Ages 13–15: Begin developing basic jump setting technique with focus on body control, consistent contact point, and landing balance.

For Ages 16–18: Master advanced jump setting, including approach variations, setting while drifting, and integrating attacking options.

Effective jump setting creates significant competitive advantages by speeding up your offense and forcing middle blockers to hesitate, giving your hitters cleaner attack opportunities against fewer organized blocks.

Deceptive Setting and Attacking

Strategic deception creates defensive uncertainty:

- **Body position consistency:** Maintain identical body positioning regardless of intended set location, removing pre-set cues.
- **Hand position disguise:** Minimize hand positioning cues that might telegraph set direction.
- **Visual deception:** Use eye focus and head position to mislead blockers about intended set targets.

- **Attack integration:** Develop effective attacking techniques (dumps, tips, attacks) that create hesitation from opposing blockers.

The more deceptive your setting technique, the fewer organized blockers your hitters will face, directly increasing kill percentage with each point of deception you develop.

Quick Wins for Advanced Techniques

- Develop a consistent jump setting approach similar to attacking.
- Practice identical body positioning for different set locations.
- Learn basic setter attack options for scoring opportunities.
- Develop a comfortable hand position for back-setting.
- Practice setting from progressively more challenging court positions.

SETTING WITHIN DIFFERENT OFFENSIVE SYSTEMS

As players advance, they encounter increasingly sophisticated offensive systems. Understanding these systems helps setters fulfill their responsibilities within team frameworks.

4-2 System (4 Hitters, 2 Setters)
Pros:

- simpler system to learn and implement
- always have a front-row setter
- easier rotation transitions

Cons:

- only 2 front-row hitters when setter is front row
- limited specialization for setters

5-1 System (5 Hitters, 1 Setter)
Pros:

- maximum setter specialization
- consistent set delivery
- strategic flexibility

Cons:

- complex transitions
- back-row setting in 3 rotations
- higher setter skill requirement

6-2 System (6 Hitters, 2 Setters Who Attack)
Pros:

- always 3 front-row hitters
- attack-focused system
- balanced offense

Cons:

- no setter specialization
- complex transitions
- back-row setting requires higher passing precision

For Ages 10–12: If using a 4-2 system, focus on basic positional understanding and simple setting targets. Emphasize consistent locations rather than complex patterns.

For Ages 13–15: Establish more detailed system responsibilities, including specific setting locations from different rotations and transition patterns.

For Ages 16–18: Master advanced system implementation, including rotation-specific quick attacks, strategic distribution patterns based on opposing blockers, and sophisticated transition sequences.

Each offensive system creates different advantages, with 5-1 systems typically offering 25-30% faster setter skill development while 6-2 systems can increase attack efficiency through consistent front-row attacking options.

Position-Specific Setting Responsibilities

The setter's responsibilities extend beyond delivering the ball to attackers:

- **Defensive responsibilities:** Master specific defensive techniques, including blocking, digging, and emergency ball handling based on rotational position.
- **Transition footwork:** Develop efficient movement patterns from defensive positions to setting locations with minimal wasted motion.
- **Offensive organization:** Thoroughly understand the team's offensive system, including rotational responsibilities, attack patterns, and strategic priorities.

Teams with well-coordinated setter transitions show approximately 30% higher side-out percentages when setters properly implement system adjustments based on defensive alignments.

Quick Wins for Systems Understanding

- Master court movement patterns specific to each rotation.
- Understand setting positions and responsibilities for each system.
- Practice smooth transitions between roles (setting, attacking, defending).
- Develop communication patterns specific to each offensive system.
- Learn how each system affects distribution options and patterns.

MENTAL ASPECTS OF SETTING

The mental and emotional components of setting often determine success more than physical skills. Developing a setter's mindset creates consistency under pressure and supports continuous improvement.

Decision-Making Under Pressure

Effective setters make quality decisions despite competitive pressure through:

- **Processing speed:** Rapidly assess multiple information inputs (pass quality, blocker positions, hitter availability) before making setting decisions.
- **Decision hierarchy:** Establish clear decision priorities that create automatic response patterns in high-pressure situations.

- **Situational awareness:** Incorporate score, momentum, and previous play outcomes into decision-making processes.

For Ages 10–12: Focus on simple decision frameworks that emphasize fundamental execution over complex strategy.

For Ages 13–15: Establish more sophisticated decision processes that incorporate multiple factors, including pass quality, hitter positions, and previous success patterns.

For Ages 16–18: Master complex decision-making, including rapid processing of defensive alignments, strategic context, and multiple offensive options.

Decision-making speed directly impacts offensive effectiveness, with elite setters making final set decisions approximately 0.15 seconds faster than intermediate setters, creating significant advantages in blocker reaction time.

Error Management and Resilience

Setting excellence requires effective response to inevitable errors through:

- **Error analysis:** Develop the ability to quickly identify error causes without dwelling on mistakes.
- **Refocusing techniques:** Establish specific mental routines for regaining focus after errors or disruptions.
- **Consistent routines:** Create pre-point routines that reset mental state regardless of previous outcomes.

Effective error management significantly impacts performance consistency, with setters maintaining approximately 25% higher setting accuracy following errors when using structured response patterns.

Quick Wins for Mental Development

- Establish a consistent pre-point routine to reset focus.
- Develop a specific physical cue (clap, touch the floor, etc.) to move past errors.
- Practice making setting decisions before receiving the ball.
- Maintain consistent positive communication regardless of score.
- Use simple, consistent terminology for play calls and communication.

FROM PRACTICE TO PERFORMANCE: THE SETTING JOURNEY

Setting mastery develops through consistent practice, focused feedback, and continuous refinement. Whether you're a dedicated setter or a player developing all-around skills, these principles guide effective development:

- **Technical foundation first:** Establish sound mechanical technique before tackling complex tactical elements. Perfect hand position, body alignment, and basic delivery mechanics create the foundation for all advanced skills.
- **Progressive challenge:** Systematically increase difficulty by adding movement challenges, decision-making elements, and performance pressure as foundational skills develop.
- **Feedback integration:** Actively seek and apply specific feedback about both technical execution and tactical decision-making.

- **Mental skill development:** Dedicate specific practice time to developing focus, resilience, leadership, and decision-making capabilities—not just physical techniques.

- **Game-context connection:** Continuously connect practice activities to game application, understanding how each drill or technique contributes to competitive effectiveness.

The setter is volleyball's most pivotal position, directly impacting team success across all competitive levels, with setting effectiveness accounting for approximately 40-50% of variation in team win percentages.

In the next chapter, we'll explore the explosive world of attacking—turning your well-placed sets into powerful points through technically sound and tactically smart hitting techniques.

CHAPTER 5:

ATTACKING: POWER AND PRECISION

The crowd holds its breath. A blur of motion as the hitter loads, approaches, and elevates. Then—BOOM! A thunderous kill that leaves the court shaking and teammates rushing in for high-fives. This electrifying moment is why countless young players fall in love with volleyball—the chance to soar above the net and deliver that perfect, unstoppable attack.

Yet behind those explosive kills lies a precise science: the coordinated blend of footwork, timing, body mechanics, and tactical decision-making that transforms raw athleticism into consistent point production. This chapter explores the essential elements that create powerful, effective attackers at every position and age level.

ATTACKING SKILL PROGRESSION CHECKLIST

Foundation Skills

☐ Execute proper footwork pattern appropriate to position.

- ☐ Time approach to match set trajectory.
- ☐ Develop coordinated arm swing mechanics.
- ☐ Contact ball at maximum reach height.
- ☐ Direct attacks to strategic court locations.

Movement Skills

- ☐ Transition efficiently from defensive to attacking positions.
- ☐ Adjust approach based on set location.
- ☐ Maintain directional options throughout approach.
- ☐ Develop balanced take-off and landing mechanics.
- ☐ Create consistent rhythm in attacking movements.

Ball Control Skills

- ☐ Execute various attack tempos (high, medium, quick).
- ☐ Control attack trajectory (hard-driven, roll, tip).
- ☐ Adapt to different set distances from net.
- ☐ Attack strategically to exploit defensive weaknesses.
- ☐ Handle non-ideal sets effectively.

Mental Skills

- ☐ Develop pre-attack routine to maintain focus.
- ☐ Read blockers and defensive alignment.
- ☐ Maintain confidence after errors.
- ☐ Communicate effectively with setter.
- ☐ Adapt strategy based on game situation.

THE FOUNDATION: APPROACH FOOTWORK

Effective attacking begins with proper approach mechanics. While various footwork patterns exist, all share core principles that generate maximum height and power through coordinated movement. The approach creates the foundation for an explosive vertical jump and directional control.

Standard Approach Patterns

The most common approach patterns include the following:

Four-Step Approach (Right-Handed)

1. **Preparation step (right):** a small step to initiate forward momentum
2. **Timing step (left):** a longer stride to establish rhythm and timing
3. **Penultimate step (right):** a powerful plant step that converts forward momentum to vertical
4. **Takeoff step (left):** the final step that completes the jump with both feet

Three-Step Approach (Right-Handed)

1. **Timing step (right):** the initial stride establishing rhythm
2. **Penultimate step (left):** the plant step converting momentum
3. **Takeoff step (right):** the final step completing the two-foot jump

For Ages 10–12: Focus on a simplified three-step approach with emphasis on rhythm and proper foot positioning rather than speed. Practice the approach pattern without the ball initially, then integrate with simple tossed balls.

For Ages 13–15: Develop the four-step approach with increased attention to the critical penultimate step. Work on consistent timing with various set tempos and maintaining directional options throughout the approach.

For Ages 16–18: Master advanced approach variations, including adjustments to different set locations, emergency (two-step) approaches, and transition footwork from defensive positions. Develop precise timing coordination with different setters.

Proper approach mechanics directly impact hitting effectiveness, with well-coordinated footwork potentially adding 4-6 inches to jump height compared to poorly executed approaches. That extra height can be the difference between hitting over the block or being stuffed in crucial game situations.

Position-Specific Approach Patterns

Each hitting position requires specific approach adaptations:

Outside Hitters (Position 4)

- standard approach angle of approximately 45 degrees to the net
- consistent starting position, typically near the left sideline
- ability to adjust to various set distances from the net
- terminal steps parallel to the net for maximum attack angles

Middle Blockers (Position 3)

- shorter, more explosive approach patterns
- variable approach angles based on set type (front, back, slides)
- earlier timing initiation to match quicker sets
- greater emphasis on lateral movement and quick repositioning

Opposite/Right Side Hitters (Position 2)

- approach angle typically 45 degrees from right side
- adaptations for back-row attacks from position 1
- approach adjustments for back sets
- timing variations for combination plays

Position-specific approach optimization can increase attack efficiency by 15–20%, particularly for specialized positions like middle blockers, where precise timing and footwork are essential for beating blockers to the point of attack.

🏃 From Defense to Offense: Transition Like a Pro

- **Block → approach:** Land and initiate approach within three steps.
- **First look:** Find the setter immediately after defensive action.
- **Body position:** Keep shoulders back, eyes up, ready to load.
- **Consistent pattern:** Build your full approach every time—even if you don't get set.

- **Patient timing:** Adjust speed to match pass quality and setter decision.

The critical penultimate step (second-to-last step) represents the most important element of the approach sequence. This step does the following:

- **Converts forward to vertical:** The lowered body position and elongated stride transform horizontal momentum into vertical explosion.
- **Creates optimal loading:** The slightly wider stance creates stability and loading in the hips and legs for maximum power.
- **Establishes direction:** The foot placement determines attack angle and body positioning.
- **Controls timing:** The length and speed of this step adjust timing to match different set tempos.

For all age groups, this critical step deserves special attention. Common errors include rushing through this step, failing to lower the center of gravity, or improper foot placement that reduces power transfer.

Quick Wins for Approach Footwork

- Practice consistent starting positions for each rotation.
- Focus on lowering body position during the penultimate step.
- Keep approaches straight rather than arcing toward the net.
- Adjust approach speed to match set tempo.

- Use floor markers/tape during practice to reinforce proper patterns.

THE POWER SOURCE: ARM SWING MECHANICS

A technically sound arm swing transforms approach momentum into controlled power. The sequence involves coordinated movement of multiple body segments working together to generate maximum velocity and control.

The Complete Arm Swing Sequence

Effective arm swing mechanics include:

1. **Loading phase:** Both arms extend backward during the approach, creating stretch in the chest and shoulder muscles.
2. **Double-arm lift:** Both arms swing forward and upward in synchronized motion during takeoff, creating vertical momentum.
3. **Bow-and-arrow position:** The hitting arm moves into a "cocked" position with elbow high and back while the non-hitting arm extends forward for balance.
4. **Forward rotation:** The torso rotates forward with the elbow leading the hand into contact.
5. **Contact phase:** The arm extends through contact with the hand slightly cupped, connecting with the top-back portion of the ball.
6. **Follow-through:** The arm continues in the intended direction of the hit with natural deceleration.

For Ages 10–12: Focus on the fundamental sequence with emphasis on proper contact point and basic arm positioning. Use underinflated balls or trainer balls to build confidence. Work on maintaining a high elbow position throughout the swing.

For Ages 13–15: Develop more refined mechanics, including proper torso rotation, consistent bow-and-arrow position, and follow-through direction. Introduce varied contact techniques (cross-court, line, off-speed).

For Ages 16–18: Master advanced swing mechanics, including wrist snap variations, torso rotation timing, and arm swing adaptations for different attack types. Develop the ability to disguise attack direction until the last moment.

Proper arm swing mechanics can increase ball velocity by 15–20% compared to arm-dominant swings that neglect proper body rotation and sequencing. In late-game situations, this extra power prevents defenders from making unexpected digs that can shift momentum.

Hand Contact and Ball Control

The moment of contact determines attack direction, velocity, and trajectory:

1. **Contact point:** Ideally at full extension slightly in front of the hitting shoulder, with the ball contacted on its top-back portion.

2. **Hand position:** Slightly cupped with spread fingers, creating both power and control.

3. **Wrist action:** Firm wrist with appropriate flexibility for directional control.

4. **Contact visualization:** Imagine "reaching over" the ball to create topspin rather than hitting directly behind it.

For Ages 10–12: Focus on basic contact point consistency and proper hand form. Use visual cues like targeting specific panels on the ball for contact. Emphasize clean contact over power production.

For Ages 13–15: Develop more precise hand control, including intentional directional hitting and beginning spin control. Practice contacting different portions of the ball to change attack direction.

For Ages 16–18: Master advanced contact techniques including spin variations, "heavy" versus "light" contact pressure, and attack disguise through identical pre-contact positioning.

Precise hand-to-ball contact can increase attack effectiveness by allowing hitters to exploit specific defensive vulnerabilities through controlled placement, even when facing strong blocking opposition. Sometimes, a well-placed, moderate-speed attack scores more reliably than a maximum-power swing.

Common Arm Swing Errors and Corrections

Typical attacking technique errors include:

Low Elbow Position

- **Error:** Hitting with elbow below shoulder height creates limited power and increased injury risk.
- **Correction:** Practice bow-and-arrow positioning with emphasis on high elbow. Use mirror feedback and wall shadows during practice.

Palm-Facing-Net Contact

- **Error:** Contacting with the palm directly facing the net creates push-like contact with reduced power and control.
- **Correction:** Practice "reaching over" the ball with the hand slightly angled downward at contact. Use suspended balls for contact point practice.

Incomplete Follow-Through

- **Error:** Stopping the arm motion at contact reduces power and increases shoulder stress.
- **Correction:** Emphasize complete motion through contact to intended target. Practice "painting the line" with follow-through direction.

Quick Wins for Arm Swing Mechanics

- Keep the elbow high in the bow-and-arrow position.
- Contact the ball at maximum reach height.
- Engage the entire body through coordinated rotation.
- Focus follow-through in the intended attack direction.
- Practice hand positioning with suspended balls at contact height.

ATTACKING STRATEGIES AND SHOT SELECTION

Beyond physical technique, effective attacking requires strategic decision-making that exploits opposing defensive vulnerabilities.

Reading the Block

Successful attackers gather and process blocking information before and during their approach:

1. **Pre-approach assessment:** Note blocker positioning and tendencies before beginning movement.

2. **During-approach reading:** Track blocker movement during early approach steps to identify potential vulnerabilities.

3. **Last-moment adjustment:** Make final shot selection based on blocker commitment observed during jump.

For Ages 10–12: Introduce basic concepts like "hit where blockers aren't" and identifying obvious open court areas. Focus primarily on clean contact rather than complex strategic decisions.

For Ages 13–15: Develop more nuanced block reading, including awareness of blocker body positioning, identification of seams between blockers, and recognition of blocker commitment timing.

For Ages 16–18: Master sophisticated block reading, including recognition of blocker tendencies, exploitation of specific blocker weaknesses, and deceptive attacking to manipulate blocker movement.

Advanced block reading can increase kill percentage by 10–15%, particularly against disciplined blocking teams where strategic shot selection becomes more important than raw power. When the score is 23–24, seeing and exploiting a blocker's tendency can be the difference between winning and losing the set.

Strategic Shot Options
Hard-Driven Attacks (✺)

- **Description:** power-driven attacks aimed at the court floor
- **When to use:** when facing single blocks, clear seams, or disorganized defense
- **Risk/Reward:** high reward potential with moderate risk against prepared defense

Off-Speed Attacks (🔄)

- **Description:** controlled "roll" shots with moderate pace and higher trajectory
- **When to use:** against strong blocking, defensive overcommitment, or when out-of-system
- **Risk/Reward:** medium reward with lower risk; excellent for maintaining offensive pressure

Tooling the Block (♀)

- **Description:** intentionally attacking blocker's hands for out-of-bounds deflection
- **When to use:** against aggressive blockers, when line/angle shots are covered
- **Risk/Reward:** high reward when executed properly; relatively safe compared to hitting through block

For Ages 10–12: Focus primarily on basic shot direction (left, center, right) with introduction to simple tips. Emphasize clean contact and basic directional control before introducing varied shot types.

For Ages 13–15: Develop a wider shot selection, including roll shots, controlled tips, and basic block contact. Practice intentional shot placement to specific court zones.

For Ages 16–18: Master comprehensive shot selection, including situational attacking decisions, strategic use of off-speed shots, and precise control when tooling the block. Develop the ability to disguise shot selection until the last moment.

Diverse shot selection directly correlates with higher attack efficiency, with studies showing that attackers with at least three reliable shot options typically maintain kill percentages 15–20% higher than single-option hitters. When it's 24–24, the safe shot to zone 6 often wins more games than the crowd-pleaser down the line.

Strategic Court Targeting

Beyond reacting to blockers, effective attackers target specific court locations based on:

- **Defensive formation vulnerabilities:** gaps in defensive alignment based on rotation or system
- **Individual defender weaknesses:** targeting less-skilled passers or defenders with specific passing weaknesses
- **Transition zones:** areas with unclear defensive responsibility or coverage challenges
- **Situational opportunities:** strategic targets based on game context (score, momentum, etc.)

Teams that strategically target specific court zones show significantly higher scoring efficiency than those relying solely on power, particularly against well-organized defensive systems. The most effective attackers know that placing a ball in the seam between two defenders creates digging confusion even when both players are highly skilled.

Quick Wins for Attack Strategy

- Scan the defense before starting your approach.
- Develop at least three different shot types you can execute reliably.
- Practice intentional placement to specific court zones.
- Learn to use blockers' hands strategically rather than always avoiding them.
- Communicate with setters about blocker tendencies and successful shots.

POSITION-SPECIFIC ATTACKING

Each volleyball position involves unique attacking responsibilities and techniques that contribute to balanced offensive systems.

Outside Hitter Attacking

Outside hitters (position 4) serve as primary attack options with specific attributes:

- **Consistent production:** often receiving the most sets, outsides must generate consistent kills from both good and challenged passes
- **Shot versatility:** typically developing the widest range of shot options to attack from various set locations and qualities

- **High-ball expertise:** mastery of high/slower tempo attacks that remain available even during challenging passing situations
- **Back-row attacking:** development of effective back-row attacks from position 5, creating six-rotation offensive threats

For Ages 10–12: Focus on basic outside fundamentals, including consistent high-ball approaches and fundamental arm mechanics. Develop reliable cross-court shots as the primary option, with basic line shots as an alternative.

For Ages 13–15: Develop greater shot diversity, including roll shots, sharp cross-court angles, and basic back-row attacking. Work on attacking from varied set distances from the net.

For Ages 16–18: Master advanced outside techniques, including sophisticated shot disguise, strategic shot selection based on game situation, and high-efficiency attacking from challenged passes.

Outside hitters typically account for 40–50% of team attacks across all levels of play, making technical and tactical excellence in this position crucial for overall offensive success. In tightly contested matches, teams whose outside hitters can maintain efficiency even from non-ideal passes often prevail in fifth sets when passing quality typically declines.

Middle Blocker Attacking

Middle attackers (position 3) create quick-strike options that stress opposing blockers:

- **Quick tempo attacks:** fast-paced attacks often executed before opposing blockers can fully commit

- **Spatial diversification:** attacks distributed across the net's length through various quick sets (1, 2, slides, etc.)
- **Timing precision:** extremely precise timing coordination with setters to execute faster tempo attacks
- **Transition efficiency:** quick movement from blocking to attacking positions during transition play

For Ages 10–12: Introduce basic middle concepts with simplified quick attacks focused on consistent timing rather than speed. Develop fundamental slide approaches through progressive teaching methods.

For Ages 13–15: Establish more advanced middle attacking, including faster-tempo sets, basic slides in both directions, and transition footwork from blocking to attacking.

For Ages 16–18: Master sophisticated middle techniques, including varied quick attack tempos, advanced combination plays, and high-efficiency attacking with limited preparation time.

Effective middle attacking creates significant offensive advantages even beyond direct kills, with data showing that teams with credible middle threats see outside hitting efficiency improve by 10–15% due to reduced blocking focus. A middle attacker who scores just 5–6 points per match may be creating 10+ additional points by pulling blockers away from outside hitters.

Opposite/Right Side Attacking

Opposite hitters (position 2) provide critical offensive balance:

- **Back-set attacking:** primary attackers for sets delivered behind the setter's position
- **Power production:** often prioritizing high-contact power hitting over shot diversity

- **Back-row specialization:** development of powerful back-row attacks from position 1
- **Out-of-system offense:** ability to generate offense from non-ideal sets during challenged situations

For Ages 10–12: Develop basic opposite fundamentals with emphasis on proper approach angles from the right side. Focus on consistent contact and fundamental arm mechanics before specialized techniques.

For Ages 13–15: Build more refined opposite skills, including back-set timing, basic back-row attacks, and power development through technique refinement.

For Ages 16–18: Master advanced opposite techniques, including high-efficiency cross-court attacking, sophisticated right-side shot selection, and specialized transition footwork.

A strong opposite attacker creates crucial offensive balance, making it difficult for opponents to commit defensive resources to other hitters. Teams with balanced attack distribution from both antennae typically win 15–20% more close sets than teams who rely predominantly on outside hitters.

Quick Wins for Position-Specific Attacking

- Practice approach patterns specific to your primary position.
- Develop timing coordination with setters for position-specific tempos.
- Learn transition pathways from defensive to attacking positions.
- Communicate position-specific preferences to setters.
- Understand each position's role in your team's offensive system.

ATTACKING AGAINST DIFFERENT DEFENSIVE SCENARIOS

Advanced attackers adjust their approach based on the specific defensive challenges presented.

Against Strong Blocking

When facing disciplined, effective blockers use the following tactics:

- **Shot diversification:** increased use of off-speed and placement attacks to create uncertainty
- **Timing variation:** subtle adjustments to approach timing to disrupt blocker synchronization
- **Tooling emphasis:** strategic use of blocker contact to score rather than attempting to avoid blocks entirely
- **Extreme angles:** exploitation of sharp angles that may be exposed by committed blockers

For Ages 13–15: Introduce basic concepts of attacking against blocks, including simple shot alternation and recognition of available court spaces. Develop comfort with appropriate block contact rather than block avoidance.

For Ages 16–18: Master sophisticated strategies, including blocker manipulation through approach deception, strategic use of off-speed attacks, and situation-based shot selection against different blocking tactics.

Strategic attacking against strong blocks can maintain kill efficiency at only 5–10% below normal rates, while power-only approaches typically see efficiency drop by 25–30% against quality blocking. When facing an effective double block, the ability to identify and exploit a specific blocker weakness becomes essential to maintaining offensive efficiency.

During Out-Of-System Play

When attacking from non-ideal situations:

- **Shot selection adjustment:** increased emphasis on control and court awareness rather than maximum power
- **Emergency techniques:** adaptations to approach and arm swing for challenged sets (too tight, too far off net, etc.)
- **Risk assessment:** appropriate decision-making regarding attack aggressiveness based on game context

For Ages 10–12: Focus on basic ball control when attacking challenged sets. Develop simple emergency techniques for common difficult situations like tight sets.

For Ages 13–15: Build more sophisticated out-of-system skills, including abbreviated approach patterns, modified arm swing mechanics, and fundamental decision-making about appropriate attack choices.

For Ages 16–18: Master advanced techniques for challenged situations, including complex decision trees for attack selection, precise control when attacking from significantly non-ideal positions, and strategic shot placement under duress.

The ability to attack effectively during out-of-system play often determines match outcomes at higher levels, with advanced teams typically converting 15–20% more out-of-system opportunities into points than intermediate teams. At 23–23 in the deciding set, the team that can generate offense from challenged passes almost always prevails.

Quick Wins for Situational Attacking

- Practice attacking from non-ideal sets to build adaptability.

- Develop comfort with appropriately using the block to score.
- Learn to recognize when power vs. control is needed.
- Communicate with teammates about effective strategies against specific blockers.
- Maintain aggressive mindset even in challenging situations.

MENTAL ASPECTS OF ATTACKING

The psychological components of attacking often differentiate good hitters from great ones. Developing mental skills enhances the application of physical techniques under competitive pressure.

Attacking Mindset and Confidence

Effective attackers maintain productive mental states through:

- **Aggressive base mindset:** fundamental commitment to offensive aggression rather than cautious play
- **Process-based confidence:** focus on executing proper technique rather than outcome-based thinking
- **Selective memory:** ability to quickly process and move beyond errors while building on successes
- **Productive self-talk:** maintaining internal dialogue that reinforces confidence and technical execution

For Ages 10–12: Develop basic confidence through appropriate challenge progression and success experiences. Focus on effort-based praise rather than outcome-based evaluation.

For Ages 13–15: Build more robust confidence, including basic error management techniques, simple pre-attack routines, and fundamental understanding of process-based thinking.

For Ages 16–18: Master advanced mental approaches, including sophisticated pre-attack routines, detailed error analysis without confidence disruption, and situation-based mindset adjustments.

Mental approach significantly impacts attacking consistency, with research indicating that attackers with established mental routines maintain kill efficiency approximately 10-15% higher during pressure situations than those without structured mental approaches. In championship point situations, mental resilience often proves more important than physical skill.

Error Response and Resilience

All attackers face errors, making error response critical for sustained performance:

- **Technical analysis:** brief, objective assessment of error causes without emotional judgment
- **Refocusing techniques:** specific routines that reset focus following errors
- **Constructive adaptation:** appropriate technique or strategy adjustments based on error patterns
- **Emotional regulation:** managing frustration or hesitation following errors through deliberate techniques

For Ages 10–12: Establish basic error response patterns, focusing primarily on moving forward rather than dwelling on mistakes. Develop simple refocusing cues and appropriate perspective on errors as learning opportunities.

For Ages 13–15: Build more sophisticated error management, including basic error-cause identification, established refocusing routines, and productive communication with coaches and teammates following errors.

For Ages 16–18: Master advanced resilience, including detailed error assessment without performance disruption, tested refocusing techniques for various situations, and the ability to make technical adjustments without overthinking.

Players with effective error-response routines typically maintain confidence and performance levels even after multiple attacking errors, while those without such routines often see performance deteriorate significantly after just one or two mistakes.

Quick Wins for Mental Development

- Establish a consistent pre-attack routine (2–3 specific actions).
- Create a simple physical cue (clap, touch the floor, etc.) to move past errors.
- Focus on "next point" thinking rather than dwelling on past mistakes.
- Practice self-talk that reinforces technique rather than outcomes.
- Maintain an aggressive mentality even after errors.

☂ If You Only Do One Thing as an Attacker...

- **Stay aggressive—even after errors**. Tentative hitting almost always produces worse results than committed attacking.

- **Master your approach rhythm**. Consistent footwork creates the foundation for all attacking success.

- **Learn to see the block and choose your shot**. Strategic shot selection beats raw power against good defenders.

- **Communicate your best tempo to your setter**. The ideal set height and speed vary for each hitter.

- **Place over power when it counts**. In crucial situations, controlled placement to open court scores more reliably than maximum-power swings.

FROM PRACTICE TO PERFORMANCE: THE ATTACKING JOURNEY

Attacking excellence develops through structured progression, deliberate practice, and game application. Whether you're a specialized position player or developing all-around skills, these principles guide effective attacking development:

- **Technical foundation first:** Master fundamental mechanics, including approach footwork, coordinated arm swing, and proper contact, before focusing on power production or advanced strategies.

- **Progressive power development:** Develop attacking power through properly sequenced technique rather than strength-dominant approaches. Power comes from coordination before strength.

- **Tactical evolution:** Build attacking intelligence by progressively incorporating defensive reading, strategic shot selection, and situation-based decision-making.

- **Feedback integration:** Actively use feedback from coaches, video analysis, and competitive results to guide technical refinement and tactical development.

The attacking journey combines technical precision, physical power, tactical intelligence, and mental resilience into volleyball's ultimate offensive weapon. Through dedicated development, you'll transform from simply hitting the ball to strategically attacking in ways that maximize scoring opportunities for your team.

Research consistently demonstrates that attacking efficiency serves as the strongest statistical predictor of team success across all competitive levels, with attacking effectiveness explaining approximately 45–60% of variation in match outcomes. Teams that attack efficiently in the last five points of close sets win approximately 70% of those sets.

In the next chapter, we'll explore the defensive counterpart to attacking—the art of serving. We'll examine how to develop powerful, precise serves that begin your team's defensive sequence by creating opponent passing challenges.

CHAPTER 6:
SERVING: STARTING STRONG

Every great defense starts with a serve designed to make your opponent uncomfortable.

The gym falls silent. A lone player stands at the end line, ball in hand, completely in control of the next moment. With a deep breath, she tosses, steps, and strikes—sending the ball sailing over the net with precision and purpose. The serve isn't just the action that begins each rally; it's volleyball's only truly individual skill—the one moment where success depends entirely on your preparation, technique, and mental approach.

While attackers may get the glory for thunderous kills, effective servers quietly control the match flow by creating defensive challenges, disrupting opponent patterns, and directly scoring points. A strategically placed serve can neutralize a dominant attacker, exploit a weak passer, or break a team's rhythm at a crucial moment.

This chapter explores the essential elements of effective serving: technical fundamentals, tactical strategies, and the mental approach that transforms this unique skill into a genuine offensive weapon.

SERVING SKILL PROGRESSION CHECKLIST

Foundation Skills

- ☐ Develop consistent pre-serve routine.
- ☐ Establish stable stance and body alignment.
- ☐ Execute controlled ball toss appropriate to serve type.
- ☐ Contact ball with proper hand position.
- ☐ Direct serves to strategic court locations.

Technical Skills

- ☐ Master fundamental underhand serving (younger players).
- ☐ Develop standing float serve technique.
- ☐ Progress to jump float serve mechanics.
- ☐ Implement topspin serve fundamentals.
- ☐ Advance to jump topspin serve (advanced players).

Tactical Skills

- ☐ Serve strategically to different court zones.
- ☐ Target specific opponents based on passing abilities.
- ☐ Vary serve types and locations.
- ☐ Adjust serving strategy based on game situation.
- ☐ Serve to disrupt opponent offensive patterns.

Mental Skills

- ☐ Maintain consistent focus and preparation.
- ☐ Develop effective error recovery methods.
- ☐ Adjust risk level based on game context.
- ☐ Visualize successful execution.
- ☐ Build confidence through progressive challenges.

If You Only Do One Thing as a Server...

- **Consistency beats power**: Reliable serves that stay in bounds create more value than maximum-power serves with high error rates.
- **Location beats velocity**: Strategic placement to exploit passing weaknesses typically outperforms pure speed.
- **Routine creates reliability**: Consistent pre-serve preparation directly correlates with serving performance under pressure.
- **View serving as defense initiation**: Your serve is the first action in your team's defensive sequence.
- **Match aggression to situation**: Adjust risk based on score, momentum, and opponent tendencies.

VISUAL BREAKDOWN OF SERVE TYPES

Serve type	Difficulty	Purpose	Best ages
Underhand	easy	consistency, learning mechanics	10–12
Standing float	medium	disruption, accuracy	11–16+
Jump float	medium-Hard	power + float deception	13–18
Topspin	hard	fast, diving trajectory	14–18
Jump topspin	advanced	high risk, high reward	16–18+

SERVING FUNDAMENTALS: THE BASIC TECHNIQUES

Effective serving begins with mastering fundamental techniques appropriate to your age and skill level. While advanced players may utilize powerful jump serves, developing solid mechanics with basic serves creates the foundation for all future progression.

The Underhand Serve

The underhand serve represents the entry point for beginning players, providing a simple, reliable method to put the ball in play.

Key Technique Elements
- forward stance with foot opposite hitting hand positioned slightly forward
- ball held in non-hitting hand at waist height
- hitting arm swings in pendulum motion with locked wrist
- contact made with heel of hand or closed fist
- follow-through in direction of intended target

For Ages 10–12: Focus on consistent contact and basic directional control. Emphasize the serve as a controlled start to the rally rather than an aggressive weapon. Use a shortened court distance initially if necessary before progressing to full-court serves.

For Ages 13–14: If still using underhand serves, emphasize increased consistency and specific target accuracy. Most players at this age should be transitioning to overhand serves, but underhand can remain a reliable backup for those still developing overhand technique.

While often considered a beginner's technique, a well-placed underhand serve can be surprisingly effective even at higher levels, particularly when strategically directed to exploit court positioning or disrupt defensive patterns. In crucial situations, a consistent underhand serve that stays in bounds is far more valuable than an aggressive overhand serve that results in an error.

The Standing Float Serve

The standing float serve provides the foundation for most advanced serving techniques, combining accessibility with effectiveness. This knuckleball-like serve travels with minimal spin, creating unpredictable flight paths that challenge passers.

Key Technique Elements

- balanced stance with weight initially on back foot
- ball held in non-dominant hand at chest/shoulder height
- short, consistent toss slightly in front of hitting shoulder
- firm, flat hand contact at center back of ball

- brief, controlled contact with "no-follow-through" technique
- weight transfer from back to front foot through contact

For Ages 10–13: Develop basic float serve mechanics with emphasis on consistent ball toss, proper contact point, and control over power. Begin with shorter distances as needed, then progress to full-court serves as technique improves.

For Ages 13–15: Refine float serve technique with more precise ball control, increased consistency, and targeted serving to specific court zones. Begin developing varied trajectories (flatter vs. higher serves) based on tactical situations.

For Ages 16–18: Master the standing float serve with high consistency and strategic placement. While many players transition to jump serving at this age, maintaining an effective standing float serve provides a reliable option in pressure situations.

A well-executed float serve can be more difficult to pass than power serves since its unpredictable flight path challenges even experienced passers. Teams with disciplined float servers typically force opponents into out-of-system play 15–20% more frequently than teams relying solely on power serves.

The Jump Float Serve

The jump float serve adds velocity and a more challenging angle of attack while maintaining the unpredictable movement of the standing float. This serve combines the deception of a float with the aggressive approach of a jump serve.

Key Technique Elements

- ball toss with one or two hands slightly in front of body
- two- or three-step approach similar to an attack approach
- take-off from one or both feet based on preference
- contact ball at highest comfortable reach point
- firm, flat hand contact identical to standing float technique
- minimal follow-through to produce float effect
- land in balanced position inside the court

For Ages 13–15: Introduce basic jump float mechanics for players with well-established standing float serves. Begin with a simplified approach and lower jump height, emphasizing control and proper contact before adding power.

For Ages 16–18: Develop more advanced jump float serving with increased approach speed, higher contact point, and greater velocity. Work on varied trajectories and precise targeting while maintaining the unpredictable float motion.

Jump float serves that combine adequate velocity with true float motion can significantly disrupt opponent offensive systems, with statistics showing that teams facing consistent jump float servers experience a 10–15% reduction in offensive efficiency compared to facing standing serves.

The Topspin Serve

The topspin serve generates power and predictable downward action through applied spin, creating a challenging trajectory that drops sharply as it crosses the net. This serve can be executed from a standing position or with a jump approach.

Standing Topspin Serve Elements

- athletic stance with ball held in front of body
- toss higher than float serve, allowing for hitting motion
- full arm swing similar to attacking motion
- contact with open hand and wrist snap
- follow-through to create forward rotation
- weight transfer through contact

Jump Topspin Serve Elements

- attack-like approach with typically 3–4 steps
- higher toss allowing for jumping approach
- jumping action similar to hitting approach
- arm swing matching attack mechanics
- full contact and follow-through creating significant topspin
- landing inside court in balanced position

For Ages 13–15: Begin with standing topspin fundamentals for players with appropriate arm strength. Focus on developing proper contact and spin creation before emphasizing power.

For Ages 16–18: Progress to jump topspin serving for physically prepared athletes. Develop serving approach mechanics, appropriate toss height, and controlled power. Emphasize in-bounds consistency over maximum velocity.

While often viewed as primarily a power technique, effective topspin serves are equally about control and placement. Players who can target specific zones with moderate-speed topspin serves typically score more points than those using maximum-effort serves with limited directional control.

Quick Wins for Float Serving

- Create consistent ball toss slightly in front of hitting shoulder.
- Contact ball with flat, firm hand (think "slap," not "push").
- Stop hand immediately upon contact to minimize spin.
- Focus on the contact point at the center-back of the ball.
- Maintain a consistent pre-serve routine to build reliability.

SERVING STRATEGY AND TACTICS

Effective serving extends beyond physical technique to include thoughtful strategic application. Smart servers don't just put the ball in play; they use each serve as a tactical weapon to create specific advantages.

Court Targeting Fundamentals

Strategic court targeting transforms basic serving technique into a tactical advantage:

Zone Serving

- **Zone 1 (right back):** challenges setter in 5-1 systems; exploits right-side passing weaknesses
- **Zone 5 (left back):** tests outside hitter passing; may limit attack options
- **Zone 6 (middle back):** forces middle back passer to move; disrupts middle attacker timing
- **Short serves:** targets seams between front and back row; challenges communication

- **Sideline serves:** tests lateral movement and increases error potential on wide passes

For Ages 10–12: Begin developing basic directional control with emphasis on simply keeping serves in bounds. Introduce the concept of serving to different zones without expecting precise targeting.

For Ages 13–15: Progress to intentional zone serving with increasing accuracy. Practice serving to specific court areas and begin identifying opponent passing weaknesses.

For Ages 16–18: Master strategic targeting with high-precision serving. Develop the ability to serve specific zones under pressure and adjust targeting based on opponent tendencies and game situations.

Zone-specific serving that matches team defensive strategy can increase defensive efficiency by 15–20% by forcing predictable attack patterns. At 23–23 in a deciding set, forcing the opponent to set from a specific zone often creates more value than attempting a high-risk ace serve.

Serving Situational Playbook—What to Do When...

- **Early in set** → serve safe, observe patterns
- **After a timeout** → target subs or cold players
- **23-23** → serve to known weakness, avoid risk
- **On a run** → mix up zones to keep pressure
- **Facing set point** → rely on your most consistent serve

Serving to Specific Passers

Advanced servers target specific opponents based on passing abilities:

- **Identifying weaker passers:** Observe pre-match warm-ups and early game play to identify passing technique differences among opponents.
- **Exploiting technical weaknesses:** Target players with specific passing limitations (e.g., poor platform control, limited range of motion, inconsistent footwork).
- **Pressure application:** Repeatedly serve to identified weaker passers to create psychological pressure and potential team tension.
- **Role disruption:** Target players with significant offensive responsibilities (e.g., primary attackers) to create additional physical and mental load.

For Ages 13–15: Introduce basic concept of serving to specific players, particularly those demonstrating passing challenges. Develop the ability to adjust serving targets based on coach direction.

For Ages 16–18: Implement sophisticated player targeting based on observed passing patterns and tendencies. Learn to recognize and exploit specific technical weaknesses in individual opponents.

Targeting specific passers can yield significant advantages beyond just passing disruption. Statistics show that outside hitters who are repeatedly served at experience a 10–15% reduction in attack efficiency due to the combined physical and mental demands of constant passing responsibility.

Match Context Serving

Strategic servers adjust their approach based on game context:

Early Game Serving

- Establish serving consistency to build confidence.
- Observe and identify opponent passing patterns.
- Test different serving strategies to determine effectiveness.
- Balance risk and reliability to establish early advantage.

Critical Point Serving

- Adjust risk level based on score situation.
- Target known passing weaknesses in pressure situations.
- Serve to disrupt opponent's primary offensive options.
- Maintain consistent routine despite heightened pressure.

Serving After Timeouts/Substitutions

- Target new players entering the game.
- Exploit potential communication gaps after adjustments.
- Maintain aggressive mindset after game stoppages.
- Counter opponent strategic adjustments.

Effective context-based serving decisions can significantly impact match outcomes. Teams that appropriately adjust serving risk based on score situation win approximately 60% of close sets (decided by 2–3 points) compared to teams that maintain consistent aggression regardless of context.

Quick Wins for Serving Strategy

- Observe opponent passing patterns during warm-ups.
- Develop at least two different serve types you can execute reliably.
- Target the seam between two passers to create communication challenges.
- Adjust the risk level based on the score situation.
- Maintain a consistent pre-serve routine regardless of pressure.

MENTAL ASPECTS OF SERVING

The psychological component of serving often determines success more than physical technique. As volleyball's only truly individual skill, serving creates unique mental challenges and opportunities for performance enhancement.

Pre-Serve Routine Development

Effective servers establish consistent pre-serve routines that create mental focus and physical readiness:

Routine Components

- taking position behind end line at same location each time
- controlled breathing to regulate focus and energy
- physical preparation (e.g., wiping hands, adjusting jersey)
- ball preparation (2–3 controlled bounces or spins)
- visualization of successful execution
- consistent timing between routine elements

My Pre-Serve Routine

Step 1: _____ *(e.g., bounce ball twice)*

Step 2: _____ *(e.g., breathe deeply)*

Step 3: _____ *(e.g., picture serve target)*

Cue phrase: "_____ "

Reset action: _____ *(e.g., adjust jersey)*

Personalization Elements

- individual focus techniques based on personal preference
- rhythm development matching personal tempo
- simplified or expanded routines based on individual needs
- adaptation to different competitive environments
- integration of visualization techniques appropriate to age and experience

For Ages 10–12: Develop a simple, consistent pre-serve routine focusing on basic preparation elements. Emphasize routine consistency rather than complexity.

For Ages 13–15: Refine pre-serve routine with more personalized elements and initial integration of basic visualization. Develop the ability to maintain routine consistency during pressure situations.

For Ages 16–18: Master advanced pre-serve routines incorporating sophisticated mental preparation, detailed visualization, and consistency across varied competitive environments.

Consistent pre-serve routines directly impact serving performance, with research showing that players who maintain established routines experience approximately 25% fewer serving errors in pressure situations compared to those with inconsistent preparation patterns.

Serving Mindset and Confidence

Beyond physical routine, effective servers develop productive mental approaches:

Serving Aggression Continuum

- understanding the spectrum from "just-in" safety serves to maximum-risk serves
- recognizing appropriate aggression levels for different game contexts
- adjusting mental approach based on score, momentum, and role
- developing confidence at each aggression level

Confidence Building Progression

- beginning with high-percentage serves in practice and competition
- gradually increasing difficulty as confidence develops
- developing comfort with productive serving pressure
- creating mental "anchors" for restoring confidence after errors

For Ages 10–12: Focus on basic confidence development through appropriate challenge progression. Emphasize the enjoyment of successful service rather than fear of errors.

For Ages 13–15: Build a more nuanced understanding of serving aggression levels and appropriate risk assessment.

Develop initial strategies for confidence maintenance during competitive challenges.

For Ages 16–18: Master sophisticated serving mindset, including detailed risk assessment, strategic aggression adjustment, and advanced confidence protection during high-pressure situations.

A player's serving mindset significantly impacts serving effectiveness, with studies showing that serves executed with confident, aggressive mentality (even at moderate velocity) create approximately 15–20% more reception challenges than technically similar serves performed with hesitant mentality.

Error Response and Resilience

All servers face errors, making error response critical for sustained performance:

Error Processing Framework

- brief technical assessment without emotional judgement
- simple physical reset cue (e.g., hand clap, deep breath)
- focus shift to next opportunity rather than past mistake
- maintenance of consistent routine despite previous outcome

Resilience Development Progression

- viewing errors as information rather than failure
- separating technique assessment from self-judgment
- building confidence through deliberate error response practice
- developing perspective on serving role within team context

For Ages 10–12: Establish basic error response patterns, emphasizing immediate focus shift and positive perspective. Create simple reset cues that young players can consistently implement.

For Ages 13–15: Develop more sophisticated error management, including basic technical assessment, established refocusing routines, and productive error response communication.

For Ages 16–18: Master advanced serving resilience, including detailed error assessment without confidence disruption, pressure-tested refocusing techniques, and strategic adjustments without overthinking.

Quick Wins for Serving Mentality

- Establish a consistent 3–5 step pre-serve routine.
- Create a specific reset action for use after errors.
- Focus on target selection before considering serve technique.
- Develop confidence through progressive serving challenges.
- Maintain consistent routine timing regardless of score situation.

FROM PRACTICE TO PERFORMANCE: THE SERVING JOURNEY

Serving excellence develops through structured progression, thoughtful practice design, and clear connection between training activities and competitive application.

Progressive Skill Development

Effective serving development follows a logical progression:

- **Technical foundation**: mastery of basic mechanics appropriate to age and physical development
- **Consistency development**: achievement of high success percentage with fundamental techniques
- **Control progression**: addition of directional accuracy and trajectory variation
- **Tactical integration**: implementation of strategic serving based on opponent tendencies and game context
- **Pressure application**: development of serving effectiveness under competitive and psychological pressure

This progression should inform both individual development plans and team practice design, allowing each player to advance at appropriate pace while maintaining essential foundations.

Practice Design Principles

Effective serving practice incorporates these key elements:

- **Purposeful repetition**: Each practice serve should have specific technical or tactical focus.
- **Progressive challenge**: Gradually increase difficulty through target size, distance, or performance consequences.
- **Context integration**: Practice conditions should replicate game situations and psychological factors.
- **Feedback utilization**: Provide clear, consistent feedback on both technique and outcome.
- **Game transfer:** Create a direct connection between practice activities and competitive application.

The design of serving practice significantly impacts skill development rate, with purposeful, game-connected practice producing approximately 30–40% faster improvement than traditional block practice without clear focus or progression.

Competitive Implementation

Ultimately, serving effectiveness is measured through competitive application across different contexts:

1. **Regular play**: consistent serving that initiates effective defensive sequences
2. **Critical moments**: strategic serving that creates advantages in key scoring situations
3. **Pressure response**: maintained effectiveness despite elevated psychological pressure
4. **Tactical flexibility**: adaptive serving based on opponent patterns and game situation
5. **Team integration**: serving approach that complements overall team defensive strategy

Research consistently demonstrates that serving effectiveness directly impacts overall team performance, with serving accounting for approximately 15–20% of point outcome variance across all competitive levels. Teams that excel in serving typically win 25–30% more close sets than teams with comparable skills in other areas but weaker serving performance.

The serving journey transforms a fundamental skill into a sophisticated weapon that contributes significantly to overall team success. Through dedicated development, you'll progress from simply putting the ball in play to strategically initiating your team's defensive system with each serve.

In the next chapter, we'll explore defensive skills, including digging and blocking—the techniques that allow teams to counter attacking threats and create transition scoring opportunities.

CHAPTER 7:

DEFENSIVE SKILLS-DIGGING AND BLOCKING

Every great serve is your team's first dig.

A thunderous attack hurtles toward the court at 50+ mph. In that split-second moment, a defender reacts, launching into a perfectly timed dive that transforms a certain point for the opponent into a spectacular save. The crowd erupts. Momentum shifts. This is volleyball defense at its most dramatic—the art of denying the opponent's best offensive efforts through skill, anticipation, and sheer determination.

While attacking may capture the spotlight, defensive play often determines match outcomes. Championship teams build their identity around relentless defensive effort, creating a psychological edge that demoralizes opponents. This chapter explores the essential defensive skills of digging and blocking—the techniques that keep rallies alive, neutralize powerful attacks, and create transition scoring opportunities.

DEFENSIVE SKILL PROGRESSION CHECKLIST

Foundation Skills

- ☐ Establish proper defensive posture and ready position.
- ☐ Develop efficient movement patterns to the ball.
- ☐ Master controlled body movements during defensive actions.
- ☐ Execute proper platform control for different ball trajectories.
- ☐ Implement safe landing techniques for extended defensive plays.

Digging Skills

- ☐ Perform effective forearm passing for defensive contacts.
- ☐ Execute overhead defensive techniques when appropriate.
- ☐ Develop one-arm extension plays for wide balls.
- ☐ Master diving and rolling techniques for extended coverage.
- ☐ Integrate defensive movements with court coverage system.

Blocking Skills

- ☐ Establish proper hand position and body alignment.
- ☐ Develop efficient footwork patterns along the net.
- ☐ Time block jumps appropriately to attacker approach.
- ☐ Penetrate hands over the net effectively.
- ☐ Implement appropriate block tactics for different attackers.

Mental Skills

- ☐ Maintain aggressive defensive mindset.
- ☐ Develop anticipation based on attacker tendencies.
- ☐ Respond constructively after defensive errors.
- ☐ Communicate effectively within defensive system.
- ☐ Sustain defensive intensity throughout extended play.

Defense Role by Position

Position	Primary responsibility	Secondary role
Left-back (5)	line attacks, deep angle shots	cover off-speed shots
Middle-back (6)	tips, roll shots, block deflections	coverage on middle attacks
Right-back (1)	cross-court attacks, deep serves	secondary setter (in system)
Front row	tips, over-block balls	net jousts, quick reads

THE FOUNDATION: DEFENSIVE READY POSITION

Effective defense begins with a specialized ready position that enables quick reactions to high-velocity attacks. While similar to the passing ready position, defensive posture incorporates subtle differences that allow for explosive movements in any direction.

Basic Defensive Stance

The fundamental defensive position includes:

- **Foot position:** feet slightly wider than shoulder width with weight distributed evenly
- **Knee bend:** deep knee flex creating a lower center of gravity than passing stance

- **Hip position:** hips lower than passing position to enable quick lateral movements
- **Weight distribution:** weight forward on the balls of the feet, never flat-footed
- **Arm position:** arms extended forward and out, already in position for platform formation
- **Hand position:** hands already separated and prepared for quick defensive reactions
- **Eye focus:** vision directed at attacker's arm swing and contact point

For Ages 10–12: Focus on basic athletic stance with emphasis on bent knees and weight forward. Simplify arm requirements to focus primarily on stable body position and movement readiness.

For Ages 13–15: Refine defensive posture with deeper knee bend, lower center of gravity, and proper arm extension. Begin developing position differences based on defensive role and court location.

For Ages 16–18: Master advanced ready position details including pre-contact weight shifts, subtle hand positioning variations, and specific adjustments based on attacker and blocker tendencies.

A properly executed defensive stance directly impacts reaction time, with players in optimal ready position typically responding 0.1–0.2 seconds faster than those in suboptimal stance—a difference that determines whether a hard-driven ball is dug or scores.

Position-Specific Defensive Postures

Defensive ready position varies based on court location and defensive role:

Front-Row Defense

- slightly higher stance to enable quick blocking movements
- arms positioned for immediate upward blocking movement
- vision divided between ball and opposing setter
- position adjusted based on blocking responsibilities

Middle Back Defense

- lower stance enabling multi-directional movement
- platform already partially formed for immediate reaction
- primary responsibility for tips and quick attacks
- position adjusted based on blocker locations

Wing Defense (Positions 1 and 5)

- deep knee bend for explosive lateral and forward movements
- extended platform preparation for wide range balls
- angled stance based on attack tendencies
- position adjusted based on block formation and opponent patterns

For Ages 10–12: Introduce basic positional differences focused primarily on court location rather than specialized techniques. Emphasize general defensive principles applicable across positions.

For Ages 13–15: Develop more specific positional techniques with increased attention to role-based ready positions. Begin integrating defensive positioning with blocking systems and court coverage patterns.

For Ages 16–18: Master sophisticated position-specific defensive stances with detailed adjustments based on opponent tendencies, teammate block formations, and tactical defensive strategies.

Position-specific defensive posture optimization can increase a team's defensive conversion rate (successful digs leading to effective counter-attacks) by 15–20%, significantly improving overall scoring efficiency.

Quick Wins for Defensive Ready Position

- Drop lower than your passing stance—defense requires a deeper knee bend.
- Keep weight forward on the balls of the feet for immediate movement.
- Pre-form your defensive platform for faster reaction.
- Focus eyes on the attacker's arm/shoulder, not the ball.
- Make stance adjustments based on your specific court position.

DIGGING TECHNIQUES: WHEN THE ATTACK COMES

Digging—the art of defending against attacks—requires specialized techniques that handle high-velocity balls while creating playable second contacts.

Platform Digging Fundamentals

The defensive platform adapts the basic passing platform with modifications for attack defense:

- **Platform angle:** generally directed more upward than passing platform to control high-velocity balls
- **Arm position:** slightly straighter arms creating firmer platform for impact absorption
- **Upper body position:** more forward lean than passing position to counter downward ball trajectory
- **Platform "give":** subtle absorption through legs and upper body while maintaining platform stability
- **Redirect control:** using controlled platform to direct ball to target rather than simply stopping forward momentum

For Ages 10–12: Focus on basic platform stability and proper body positioning behind the ball. Use slower-paced attacks and controlled drills to build fundamental digging mechanics.

For Ages 13–15: Develop more refined platform control, including angle adjustments for different attack velocities and trajectories. Begin incorporating movement challenges and realistic attack speeds.

For Ages 16–18: Master advanced platform techniques, including subtle angle variations based on attack types, blocker touches, and strategic target locations.

Proper platform digging technique allows defenders to control hard-driven attacks while creating playable second contacts, with advanced technique reducing "wild digs" by approximately 30–40% compared to improper platform formations.

Digger's Quick Checklist
- lower than your serve receive stance
- eyes on arm, not ball
- platform angle = up, not out
- expect every ball—even blocked ones
- dive with direction, not desperation

Overhead Defensive Techniques
While platform digging forms the foundation of defense, overhead techniques provide important alternatives for specific situations:

- **Overhead digging:** using setting form to control higher attacks or balls deflected by blockers
- **Hand defense:** single or double-hand deflections for balls too fast for platform formation
- **Extension plays:** reaching beyond normal platform range with one-arm extensions
- **Emergency techniques:** using any legal body surface to prevent ball from touching court

For Ages 13–15: Introduce basic overhead defensive techniques primarily for higher contacts and deflected balls. Develop fundamental understanding of when different techniques are appropriate.

For Ages 16–18: Master advanced overhead defense, including split-second technique selection, controlled single-hand deflections, and strategic use of emergency defensive methods.

Note: For players under 13, the focus should remain on fundamental platform digging before introducing overhead variations.

Effective integration of different defensive techniques can increase defensive efficiency by 15–20%, particularly against sophisticated offenses that use varied attack speeds and placements.

Movement to the Ball: Defensive Footwork

Defensive footwork differs from passing movement due to:

- higher ball velocities requiring explosive first-step movement
- multi-directional response patterns
- need for extended coverage through diving/rolling techniques
- recovery requirements after defensive actions

Key defensive movement principles include:

- **First-step explosion:** immediate power step in ball direction
- **Direct path:** most efficient line to intercept ball trajectory
- **Body position maintenance:** keeping shoulders and hips facing the attack through movement
- **Extension preparation:** movement patterns that enable controlled extension when needed
- **Recovery speed:** quick return to defensive position after play

For Ages 10–12: Develop basic defensive movement with emphasis on quick first step and direct path to the ball. Introduce fundamental diving and extension concepts through progressive drills.

For Ages 13–15: Refine defensive footwork with increased speed and multi-directional capabilities. Develop controlled diving techniques and basic recovery movements.

For Ages 16–18: Master advanced defensive movements including complex read-and-react patterns, specialized extension techniques, and high-efficiency recovery systems.

Floor Defense Techniques

Extended defensive plays require specialized techniques for reaching balls beyond normal stance range:

Controlled Extension Steps

- extended lateral reaching while maintaining balance
- one-foot power step creating extended reaching range
- platform adjustments for extended position contacts

Basic Diving Technique

- forward movement with controlled lowering of center of gravity
- platform extension with one arm leading for extended reach
- controlled chest slide with body weight on platform arm
- free arm used for balance and court contact control

Shoulder Roll Technique

- used for balls requiring greater extension than standard dive
- forward diving motion with shoulder rotation during contact
- rolling motion to distribute impact and enable quick recovery
- controlled platform presentation during rolling sequence

For Ages 10–12: Introduce basic extension steps and fundamental diving progressions using mats and controlled environments. Focus on proper technique and safety before emphasizing extended defensive plays.

For Ages 13–15: Develop more complete diving and rolling techniques with gradual progression from controlled practice to game-like application. Begin connecting extension techniques to defensive court coverage.

For Ages 16–18: Master advanced floor defense, including situation-specific technique selection, high-efficiency recovery movements, and integration of extended plays within overall defensive system.

Teams with well-developed floor defense capabilities typically convert 20–25% more "out-of-system" plays into points, creating a significant advantage in closely matched competitions.

Quick Wins for Digging Technique

- Angle your platform slightly upward for hard-driven balls.
- Create a slightly firmer platform than when passing serves.
- Stay low through your defensive movement.

- Keep eyes focused on the attacker's arm/shoulder for earlier read.
- Use legs to absorb impact while maintaining platform stability.

BLOCKING FUNDAMENTALS: THE FIRST LINE OF DEFENSE

Blocking serves as volleyball's first line of defense, creating a vertical barrier that contains attacking options and creates defensive advantages for floor defenders.

Basic Blocking Position

Effective blocking begins with proper hand and body positioning:

- **Hand position:** hands held at upper forehead height with fingers spread and wrists firm
- **Arm alignment:** elbows pointed outward creating maximum lateral blocking surface
- **Shoulder position:** shoulders raised ("shrugged") to protect neck and create higher blocking surface
- **Body alignment:** body positioned perpendicular to net with feet shoulder-width apart
- **Weight distribution:** weight balanced and slightly forward for immediate jumping action

For Ages 10–12: Focus on basic hand and arm positions with minimal emphasis on actual blocking contact. Develop fundamental understanding of blocking purpose and basic positioning near the net.

For Ages 13–15: Refine blocking stance with proper hand position, arm extension, and initial footwork. Begin developing actual blocking timing against controlled attacks.

For Ages 16–18: Master detailed blocking position, including subtle hand and arm alignments, weight distribution variations based on attacking tendencies, and position adjustments for different offensive systems.

Proper base blocking position creates the foundation for all blocking actions and significantly impacts blocking effectiveness by ensuring optimal hand placement and body alignment for maximum court coverage.

Blocking Footwork

Efficient movement along the net determines blocking effectiveness:

Basic Blocking Steps

- **Shuffle step:** Small, quick lateral steps maintaining facing-the-net orientation
- **Crossover step:** Larger lateral movement crossing one foot over the other
- **Slide step:** Quick sliding movement for single-step adjustments

Footwork Patterns

- **Middle blocker lateral movement:** Explosive side-to-side movement covering wide court areas
- **Outside/Opposite transition:** Movement from defensive to blocking positions

- **Closing movement:** Quick adjustment steps to create double blocks

For Ages 10–12: Develop basic lateral movement along the net with emphasis on balance and direction rather than speed. Introduce fundamental crossover and shuffle techniques.

For Ages 13–15: Refine blocking footwork with increased speed and directional variations. Develop more specific position-based movement patterns, including middle blocker lateral techniques.

For Ages 16–18: Master advanced blocking movements, including high-speed lateral adjustments, complex transition footwork, and rapid closing movements for double-blocking formations.

Efficient blocking footwork directly impacts defensive success rates, with well-coordinated blocking movements increasing successful block touches by 15-20% compared to delayed or imbalanced footwork patterns.

Blocking Timing and Execution

Effective blocks result from precise timing and proper execution:

1. **Read phase:** observing setter and preparation for attacker approach
2. **Movement phase:** efficient footwork to ideal blocking position
3. **Loading phase:** balanced pre-jump position with hands in ready position
4. **Jumping phase:** vertical explosion timed to attacker approach

5. **Penetration phase:** active reaching over and across net at peak height

6. **Landing phase:** balanced recovery maintaining defensive readiness

For Ages 10–12: Focus primarily on basic jump timing and hand position rather than complex reading or penetration techniques. Develop fundamental understanding of when to jump in relation to attacker.

For Ages 13–15: Refine blocking timing with increased attention to attacker approach reading and basic penetration concepts. Begin developing more sophisticated block timing against varied attack tempos.

For Ages 16–18: Master advanced blocking execution, including split-second timing adjustments, situational penetration variations, and complex reading of different offensive systems and attackers.

Precise block timing creates significantly more defensive advantages than pure physical attributes, with well-timed blocks from average-height players typically outperforming poorly-timed blocks from taller players.

Block Types and Strategies

Block type	Use when...
Commit block	quick middle attacks or dominant hitters
Read block	versus varied offenses; need flexibility
Swing block	when moving late or over longer distances
Soft block	against crafty hitters; want controlled deflection

Tactical Considerations

- **Seam responsibility:** Proper hand placement relative to blocking partners
- **Net assignment:** Strategic decisions about which attackers receive doubled blocks
- **Court coverage integration:** Coordination between block formation and floor defender positioning

For Ages 13–15: Introduce basic blocking tactics with emphasis on proper positioning relative to attackers. Begin developing fundamental understanding of how blocking integrates with floor defense.

For Ages 16–18: Master advanced blocking strategy, including sophisticated block assignment systems, situational tactics against different offensive strategies, and coordinated blocking schemes integrated with defensive specialists.

Note: For players under 13, tactical blocking concepts should be minimized in favor of fundamental technique development.

Strategic blocking significantly impacts overall defensive effectiveness, with coordinated blocking systems increasing team defensive efficiency by 20–30% compared to individual blocker decision-making.

Quick Wins for Blocking

- Position hands at forehead height with fingers spread and firm.
- Keep eyes on the setter until the set is made, then attacker.
- Press hands over the net at the peak of your jump.
- Maintain firm wrists and shoulders when penetrating.
- Land in a balanced position ready for transition.

MENTAL ASPECTS OF DEFENSE

The psychological component of defense often determines success more than physical technique, particularly during extended rallies and pressure situations.

Defensive Mindset Development

Effective defenders cultivate specific mental approaches:

- **Relentless pursuit mentality:** fundamental belief that no ball is unplayable
- **Positive expectation:** assumption of successful defensive outcome
- **Present-moment focus:** attention directed entirely to current defensive responsibility
- **Process orientation:** emphasis on proper technique execution rather than outcome
- **Collective responsibility:** recognition of defense as shared team commitment

For Ages 10–12: Develop basic defensive mentality emphasizing effort and ball pursuit. Create positive associations with defensive plays through enthusiastic recognition and celebration.

For Ages 13–15: Build more sophisticated defensive mindset, including resilience after errors, connection between defensive effort and team success, and personal defensive identity development.

For Ages 16–18: Master advanced defensive psychology, including performance under pressure, maintenance of defensive intensity during extended competitions, and leadership within defensive systems.

A team's defensive mindset directly impacts match outcomes, with teams exhibiting strong defensive mentality winning approximately 65–70% of extended rallies (10+ contacts) regardless of relative physical tools or technical skill levels.

Reset Between Rallies

1. Touch knees → Get low
2. Clap once → Refocus eyes on attacker
3. Say your assignment out loud

Anticipation and Reading Skills

Beyond physical positioning, defenders must develop perceptual skills:

- **Attacker tendency recognition:** identifying individual hitting patterns and preferences
- **Pre-contact cues:** observing attacker approach, body positioning, and arm preparation
- **Set trajectory reading:** evaluating set quality and location to anticipate attack options
- **Blocker evaluation:** assessing likely block formation and potential deflection patterns
- **System recognition:** identifying opponent offensive patterns and tendencies

For Ages 13–15: Begin developing basic anticipation skills focused primarily on obvious attacker cues and fundamental pattern recognition. Introduce the concept of reading opponent tendencies.

For Ages 16–18: Master advanced reading skills, including subtle pre-contact indicators, complex offensive pattern recognition, and anticipatory positioning based on multi-factor analysis.

Note: For players under 13, reading skills should emerge naturally through play rather than explicit instruction, with primary focus remaining on fundamental techniques and effort.

Developed reading abilities can improve defensive reaction time by 0.1–0.3 seconds—a critical margin that often determines whether attacks are successfully defended or score directly.

Quick Wins for Defensive Mentality

- Adopt the "no ball hits the ground" mindset in every practice.
- Celebrate teammate defensive efforts as enthusiastically as kills.
- Focus on proper defensive positioning before the attack occurs.
- Create a physical "reset" cue to move past defensive errors.
- Communicate defensive responsibilities before each play.

FROM PRACTICE TO PERFORMANCE: THE DEFENSIVE JOURNEY

Defensive excellence develops through structured progression, deliberate practice design, and clear connection between training activities and competitive application.

"Effortful defense wins the 30-second rallies that decide the match."

The defensive journey transforms reaction-based skills into anticipatory excellence that frustrates opponents and energizes teammates. Through dedicated development, you'll progress from simply trying to keep the ball off the floor to strategically controlling opponent attacks in ways that create transition scoring opportunities for your team.

Research consistently shows that teams with superior defensive efficiency win approximately 65–70% of closely contested matches (decided by 5 or fewer points per set) even when attacking and serving statistics are relatively equal. Defense truly forms the foundation of volleyball excellence at every level of competition.

"The team that digs more wins more—regardless of how flashy their offense looks."

In the next chapter, we'll explore team systems and tactics—the frameworks that integrate individual skills into coordinated team performance that maximizes strengths and minimizes vulnerabilities.

CHAPTER 8:
TEAM SYSTEMS AND TACTICS

In volleyball, 1+1+1+1+1+1 = infinity.
When systems click, teams do the impossible.

Six players become one on the volleyball court. Individual skills matter, but in volleyball, the magic happens when those skills combine into a unified system where every player knows their role, anticipates teammates' movements, and executes seamlessly as a collective force.

This chapter explores the tactical frameworks that transform talented individuals into championship teams—the offensive and defensive systems that create predictable patterns from chaos, maximize player strengths, and create scoring opportunities through coordinated team play.

TEAM SYSTEMS SKILL PROGRESSION CHECKLIST

Foundation Skills
☐ Understand basic 6-6 rotational principles.

- ☐ Learn positional responsibilities in each rotation.
- ☐ Execute basic transition patterns between offense and defense.
- ☐ Communicate effectively within system requirements.
- ☐ Adapt individual skills to team tactical needs.

Offensive System Skills

- ☐ Master serve-receive patterns for chosen system.
- ☐ Execute position-specific attacking responsibilities.
- ☐ Understand quick attack timing and combination plays.
- ☐ Transition efficiently from defense to organized offense.
- ☐ Adjust offensive approach based on opponent defense.

Defensive System Skills

- ☐ Implement base defensive formations.
- ☐ Execute rotation-specific defensive assignments.
- ☐ Coordinate blocking patterns with back-row coverage.
- ☐ Transition from blocking to attacking positions.
- ☐ Adapt defensive coverage based on opponent tendencies.

Advanced Tactical Skills

- ☐ Read and counter opponent offensive systems.
- ☐ Implement specialized defensive adjustments.
- ☐ Execute multiple offensive systems within matches.
- ☐ Manage strategic timeouts and substitutions.
- ☐ Lead system implementation and adjustment.

ROTATION SYSTEM CHEAT SHEET

System	Number of setters	Attack options	Complexity	Best for
6-6	0 dedicated	balanced	low	Ages 10–12
4-2	2 (front row)	limited	medium	Ages 10–14
5-1	1	complex	high	Ages 13–18
6-2	2 (back row)	high	high	Ages 14–18

THE 6-6 FOUNDATION: WHERE IT ALL BEGINS

All volleyball systems begin with understanding the 6-6 rotational pattern—the basic framework where all six players play all positions as they rotate through the court. This foundation serves two crucial purposes: it develops well-rounded players who understand all positions and creates a base from which more specialized systems can evolve.

In the 6-6 system, players truly experience volleyball from every angle. When you're in the front row, you learn the nuances of blocking and quick attacking. When you rotate to the back row, you gain appreciation for defensive positioning and back-court attacks. This comprehensive exposure creates players who understand how their individual actions impact the entire team structure.

Key 6-6 Principles

Understanding positional responsibilities forms the core of 6-6 success. Each position has specific requirements, but the beauty of this system lies in its balanced development approach. Players learn that effective rotation isn't just about clockwise movement—it's about maintaining court coverage, communication, and spacing throughout the transition.

- **For Ages 10–12:** Master basic rotational understanding with simplified responsibilities. Focus on knowing where to go next and basic position functions rather than complex tactical elements.

- **For Ages 13–15:** Develop deeper positional awareness with increased responsibility in serve-receive, blocking, and attacking. Begin understanding how individual rotations create team advantages.

- **For Ages 16–18:** Refine 6-6 execution with advanced positional understanding, serving as foundation for more complex systems. Develop leadership in helping teammates understand rotational requirements.

Teams that master 6-6 fundamentals before advancing to specialized systems typically show 25–30% faster adaptation to complex offensive and defensive patterns.

STANDARD COMMUNICATION CALLS

Situation	Call	Meaning
Serve receive	"Mine"	I'm taking this pass
	"Help"	I need assistance on this pass
	"Out"	Ball is going out of bounds
Blocking	"With"	I'm blocking with you
	"Solo"	I'm blocking alone
	"Switch"	Change blocking assignment

Defense	"Short"	Prepare for tip or short shot
	"Line"	Ball likely going down the line
	"Deep"	Ball likely going to back court
Transition	"Go"	Run offensive play
	"Free"	Easy ball coming over
	"Cover"	Get ready for block coverage

OFFENSIVE SYSTEMS: CREATING SCORING OPPORTUNITIES

Effective offensive systems create predictable patterns that enable setters to distribute efficiently while maximizing attacker strengths. Each system represents a tactical choice that influences practice structure, player development, and game strategy.

The 5-1 System: Specialized Setting

The 5-1 system features one setter and five hitters, creating consistent setting throughout all rotations. This specialization allows for the most sophisticated offensive development, as the setter can build chemistry with all attackers while hitters focus purely on attacking responsibilities.

5-1 Advantages

The primary benefit of the 5-1 lies in its consistency—having the same setter throughout all rotations creates predictable timing and preferred delivery for each attacker. This consistency enables more complex offensive patterns, including intricate quick attacks and combination plays that require precise timing between setter and hitter.

5-1 Challenges

The complexity of the 5-1 emerges in the setter's varied responsibilities across rotations. When serving from the back row, setters must cover significant distance to reach setting position, requiring excellent conditioning and court awareness. Front-row rotations present different challenges, as the setter must balance blocking responsibilities with offensive leadership.

Rotation-Specific Considerations

Each rotation presents unique challenges and opportunities within the 5-1 framework:

- **Rotation 1 (Front-right setter):** excellent back-set opportunities, but blocking responsibilities against opponent outside hitters demand attention
- **Rotation 2 (Front-middle setter):** balanced attack options with both quick attacks and outside sets readily available
- **Rotation 3 (Front-left setter):** superior angle for back sets, specific blocking adjustments needed
- **Rotation 4 (Back-left setter):** maximum distance for setting offers complete range of options but requires excellent movement efficiency
- **Rotation 5 (Back-middle setter):** excellent court vision creates opportunities for tactical distribution

- **Rotation 6 (Back-right setter):** minimal setting distance combines with optimal court coverage for consistent execution

For Ages 13–15: Introduce basic 5-1 concepts with simplified setter responsibilities. Focus on fundamental setting positions and basic attack patterns.

For Ages 16–18: Master advanced 5-1 implementation including rotation-specific quick attacks, combination plays, and strategic distribution patterns.

The 6-2 System: Attack-Focused Offense

The 6-2 utilizes two setters who attack when front-row and set when back-row, maintaining three front-row attackers always. This system prioritizes offensive balance while creating unique tactical challenges.

6-2 Advantages

Having three front-row attackers in every rotation creates the broadest offensive front possible. This numerical advantage forces opponents to spread their blocking coverage, often creating one-on-one blocking situations that favor attackers.

6-2 Challenges

The primary challenge lies in maintaining setting consistency with two different setters. Each setter-hitter relationship requires separate development, and attackers must adjust to potentially different setting styles throughout rotations.

Key 6-2 Transition Patterns

Understanding transition patterns becomes crucial for 6-2 success. The movement from setter attack position to setting position must occur seamlessly, often under time pressure.

The 4-2 System: Developmental Foundation

The 4-2 system uses four attackers and two setters, with setting responsibilities alternating between rotations. This system serves as an excellent bridge between 6-6 and more specialized systems.

4-2 Advantages

Simplicity characterizes the 4-2's primary advantage. With always having a front-row setter, transitions remain straightforward, and players can focus on fundamental execution rather than complex movement patterns.

4-2 Challenges

Offensive limitation emerges as the primary challenge, with only two front-row attackers when the setter occupies a front-row position. This reduction sometimes allows opponents to concentrate blocking more effectively.

For Ages 10–12: Focus on basic 4-2 implementation with emphasis on positional understanding rather than complex offensive patterns.

For Ages 13–15: Develop more sophisticated 4-2 execution with increased attack variety and basic combination plays.

Quick Wins for Offensive Systems

- Master your position's specific responsibilities in each rotation.
- Communicate consistently with your setter about preferred tempos.
- Run full approach patterns even when not getting set.
- Support transitioning teammates with coverage calls.
- Develop at least 2–3 go-to plays within your system.

DEFENSIVE SYSTEMS: CONTROLLING OPPONENT ATTACK

Effective defensive systems coordinate blocking and floor defense to limit opponent scoring opportunities. These systems must account for individual player abilities while creating cohesive court coverage.

Team Blocking Concepts

Blocking assignments form the foundation of defensive systems:

- **Man-to-man blocking:** Each blocker assumes responsibility for a specific attacker, moving with them regardless of court position. This approach creates individual accountability and often produces cleaner blocking technique.
- **Area blocking:** Blockers take responsibility for court zones rather than specific players. This system often produces better transition speed and simplified movement patterns.
- **Combination blocking:** The most sophisticated approach, blending man-to-man and area concepts

based on situation and rotation. This flexibility requires advanced tactical understanding.

Block Coverage Schemes

Floor defense integration with blocking creates the complete defensive picture:

- **2-1-3 formation:** Two players move up for short deflections, one player covers middle depth, and three players maintain deeper court coverage. This formation balances tip coverage with power ball defense.

- **1-5 formation:** One player covers close to blockers while five maintain deeper positions. This scheme prioritizes hard-driven ball coverage while accepting risk on shorter deflected balls.

- **2-4 formation:** Two blockers pull off to cover deflections, four back-row defenders maintain deeper court coverage. This balanced approach works well against varied offenses.

Back-Row Defense Integration

Defensive specialist roles create specialized court coverage:

- **Targeted passing responsibilities:** Specific players assume primary passing duties, allowing others to focus on pure defense. This specialization often improves overall defensive efficiency.

- **Court coverage assignments:** Detailed zone responsibilities ensure complete court coverage while minimizing overlap. These assignments must adjust based on blocking formation and opponent tendencies.

Floor Defense Patterns
Base Defense Positioning

Understanding where to position before attacks determines defensive success. Base positions establish starting points from which players adjust based on visual cues and attack development.

Defensive Adjustments

- Setter dump coverage presents a unique challenge requiring specific attention.
- Quick attack considerations influence defensive positioning and timing.
- Out-of-system defensive shifts create temporary vulnerabilities.
- Deep court protection ensures coverage against powerful attacks.

For Ages 10–12: Focus on basic defensive positioning and simple zone coverage concepts.

For Ages 13–15: Develop more sophisticated defensive assignments with increased coordinated coverage patterns.

For Ages 16–18: Master advanced defensive systems, including multiple coverage options and seamless defensive-to-offensive transitions.

Teams implementing coordinated defensive systems typically reduce opponent attack efficiency by 15–20% while increasing their own transition scoring by 25–30%.

STRATEGIC GAME MANAGEMENT

Beyond implementing basic systems, successful teams must manage strategic elements that influence match outcomes.

Timeout Tactical Reset Checklist

1. Call one key change (offense or defense).
2. Re-center the team emotionally.
3. Clarify next rotation responsibilities.
4. Set a one-point goal.

Timeout Usage Strategy

Strategic timeout application requires understanding momentum shifts and system requirements:

- **Momentum management:** Recognizing when opponent runs exceed normal variance helps determine timeout timing. Teams often benefit from timeouts during 3+ point opponent runs.

- **System breakdown corrections:** When defensive or offensive patterns fail repeatedly, timeouts provide opportunity for tactical adjustments and refocusing.

- **Strategic score adjustments:** Key scoring situations (20-20 or similar) often benefit from timeouts for final strategic alignment.

Substitution Patterns

Strategic substitution requires understanding player capabilities and match situations:

Common Substitution Strategies

- **Defensive specialist patterns:** Libero and defensive specialist entries follow specific rotational logic.
- **Serving specialist usage:** Strong servers often enter during crucial rotations where tough serves create immediate value.
- **Offensive enhancement:** Right-side and opposite hitter substitutions often emphasize attacking ability over defensive prowess.
- **Rest management:** Planned rotational rest prevents fatigue during tournaments or long matches.

ADAPTATION AND COUNTER-STRATEGY

Effective teams don't just execute their own systems; they adapt to counter opponent strengths and exploit weaknesses.

Scouting Integration
Key Scouting Elements

Understanding opponent patterns creates a foundation for tactical adaptation:

- **Opponent serving patterns:** identifying preferred serving zones and pressure-situation tendencies
- **Offensive system identification:** recognizing whether opponents utilize 5-1, 6-2, or modified systems

- **Key player tendencies:** identifying individual attacker preferences and setter distribution patterns
- **Defensive coverage preferences:** understanding how opponents organize their defense

In-Match Adjustments

Tactical Adaptation Process

Successful adaptation follows systematic recognition and implementation:

1. **Recognition phase:** quickly identify emerging patterns or opponent adjustments
2. **Analysis phase:** determine effective counter-strategies
3. **Communication phase:** clear, concise relay of adjustments
4. **Implementation phase:** disciplined execution of tactical modifications
5. **Evaluation phase:** continuous assessment of adjustment effectiveness

For Ages 13–15: Introduce basic scouting concepts and simple adjustments.

For Ages 16–18: Develop sophisticated scouting integration, including complex counter-strategies and in-match adjustments.

MENTAL ASPECTS OF TEAM PLAY

System Discipline

Effective teams maintain system discipline even under pressure:

- **Role acceptance:** Understanding and embracing specific responsibilities within team systems creates consistent execution. When players trust their defined roles, overall system efficiency increases significantly.

- **Pressure response:** Maintaining system integrity during critical points prevents breakdown when stakes increase. Disciplined teams execute familiar patterns automatically.

Communication Systems

On-Court Communication Patterns

Effective communication creates predictable patterns that support system execution:

- **Pre-play communication:** play calls, blocking assignments, establish tactical alignment
- **During-play communication:** help calls, coverage adjustments, maintain system organization
- **Post-play communication:** encouragement, quick feedback, help maintain positive energy
- **Between-points communication:** strategic adjustments, momentum management

Team Chemistry Within Systems
Building System Chemistry

Strong team chemistry enhances system effectiveness:

- **Consistent practice patterns:** repeated system execution creates automatic responses during competition
- **Clear role definition:** when everyone understands their specific responsibilities, trust develops naturally
- **Positive reinforcement:** celebrating system successes strengthens collective commitment

Quick Wins for Team Systems

- Know your primary responsibility in each rotation.
- Develop automatic transition patterns between phases.
- Use consistent terminology for all system calls.
- Practice system execution against varied opponent styles.
- Create backup plans for when primary systems break down.

FROM PRACTICE TO PERFORMANCE: SYSTEMS INTEGRATION

Progressive System Development

Effective system implementation follows a logical development progression:

1. **Positional understanding:** Individual players must first master their specific requirements within each system.
2. **Basic pattern execution:** Teams must develop fundamental system movements before adding complexity.

3. **Pressure integration:** Maintaining system execution under competitive pressure requires gradual exposure.

4. **Tactical flexibility:** Once basic systems function reliably, teams can implement variations.

5. **Strategic mastery:** Advanced teams lead their own system adaptation.

Practice Design for Systems

Effective System Practice

Practicing complete system patterns, rather than isolated skills, creates automatic execution:

- **Whole system integration:** drills must incorporate entire system movements

- **Pressure simulation:** creating competitive scenarios tests system integrity under stress

- **Transition practice:** quick system transitions between offensive and defensive phases require specific attention

Competitive Implementation

System Success Indicators

Evaluating system effectiveness requires understanding key performance markers:

- **Reduced transition errors:** Fewer mistakes during offensive-defensive phase changes indicate effective implementation.

- **Higher offensive efficiency:** Systematic approaches typically produce more consistent scoring opportunities.

- **Strategic adaptation speed:** Teams adept at system modification respond quickly to opponent adjustments.

Teams that effectively implement and adapt their systems typically win 60–65% of close sets (decided by 3 points or fewer) compared to teams with comparable individual skills but less systematic organization.

"When systems become second nature, teams find ways to win even on days when individual execution isn't perfect."

In the next chapter, we'll explore mental performance and leadership—the psychological foundations that enable players to execute systems effectively under pressure and lead their teams to success.

CHAPTER 9:
MENTAL PERFORMANCE AND LEADERSHIP

Champions aren't made in the gyms. Champions are made from something they have deep inside them—a desire, a dream, a vision. –Muhammad Ali

The score is 24-24 in the deciding set. The serve floats over the net, and in that moment—when the crowd noise fades and everything slows down—championship teams reveal what they're truly made of. Not their physical skills or tactical systems, but their mental strength and leadership that carries them through the pressure.

While you've mastered the physical fundamentals and tactical systems detailed in previous chapters, this chapter explores volleyball's greatest differentiator: the mental game. The psychological foundations determine who executes skills consistently under pressure, who leads teammates through adversity, and who transforms good players into champions.

MENTAL PERFORMANCE PROGRESSION CHECKLIST

Foundation Skills

- ☐ Develop consistent pre-performance routines.
- ☐ Maintain focus during individual skill execution.
- ☐ Recover quickly from individual errors.
- ☐ Apply basic visualization techniques.
- ☐ Understand personal motivation drivers.

Competition Skills

- ☐ Maintain composure under pressure.
- ☐ Execute skills consistently in competitive environments.
- ☐ Adapt performance based on game situation.
- ☐ Support teammates effectively during challenges.
- ☐ Implement strategic thinking during matches.

Leadership Skills

- ☐ Communicate effectively in pressure situations.
- ☐ Demonstrate positive energy management.
- ☐ Guide team through tactical adjustments.
- ☐ Model resilient behavior after setbacks.
- ☐ Inspire collective confidence and cohesion.

Advanced Mental Skills

- ☐ Lead strategic discussions and adjustments.
- ☐ Manage complex competitive emotions.
- ☐ Develop and execute long-term mental training.

- ☐ Create positive team culture sustainably.
- ☐ Mentor developing players in mental skills.

LEADERSHIP STYLES TABLE

Leadership type	What it looks like
Task leader	"Run that play again" / Sets team tone in drills / Focuses on execution details / First to analyze breakdowns
Social leader	"How are you feeling?" / Organizes team bonding / Maintains relationships / Helps resolve conflicts
Emotional leader	"We've got this" / Bounces back from errors visibly / Models energy management / Stays positive in adversity

MENTAL TRAINING FOUNDATIONS

Developing Volleyball IQ

Just as you learned to read blockers for attacking decisions, mental volleyball requires reading situations, teammates, and your own responses with equal precision.

Tactical Intelligence Components

- **Pattern recognition:** identifying opponent tendencies and system weaknesses
- **Situational awareness:** understanding score, rotation, and momentum context

- **Strategic thinking:** making tactical decisions that benefit team success
- **Anticipation skills:** reading plays before they develop fully
- **System understanding:** knowing how individual actions impact team performance

For Ages 10–12: Focus on basic situational awareness— understanding whether you're ahead or behind, recognizing when your team has momentum, and making simple tactical decisions like serving to open court spaces.

For Ages 13–15: Develop pattern recognition by studying specific opponents during matches. Begin understanding how score situations influence tactical choices (aggressive vs. safe serves at different points).

For Ages 16–18: Master advanced tactical intelligence, including predictive analysis based on multiple data points, strategic adaptation during matches, and leading tactical discussions with teammates and coaches.

Sample Mental Game Plan
Alex's Match Plan

- **Pre-game routine:** 3 songs + 1 deep breath + "This is my court"
- **Error reset cue:** clap hands + say "Next point"
- **Leadership action:** encourage a teammate after every play
- **Pressure response:** 2 deep breaths + focus on platform
- **Post-match review:** journal 3 learnings within 30 minutes

Research shows that athletes with personalized mental game plans perform 25–30% more consistently under pressure than those without structured mental preparation.

PRESSURE MANAGEMENT: PERFORMING WHEN IT MATTERS

Understanding Competition Anxiety

Like learning footwork patterns, understanding how your mind and body respond to pressure requires recognition and practice. Competition anxiety manifests across three domains:

Cognitive (Mind)
- racing thoughts about consequences
- difficulty concentrating on present moment
- overthinking technical movements
- catastrophic thinking patterns

Physical (Body)
- increased heart rate and breathing
- muscle tension and restriction
- energy fluctuations (too high or low)
- changes in coordination or timing

Behavioral (Actions)
- rushed decision-making
- technical execution changes
- communication pattern disruption
- avoidance of responsibility

Understanding these responses helps you recognize them early and implement appropriate management strategies.

PRESSURE PLAY PROTOCOL

Step	Action	Purpose
B reathe	Deep 4-count inhale, 4-count exhale	Regulate nervous system
R elax	Drop shoulders, release face tension	Reduce physical resistance
E yes	Focus on target or task	Direct attention productively
A ffirm	"I can do this"	Build confidence
T rust	Rely on your training	Access automatic skills
H ighlight	See the opportunity, not threat	Reframe pressure positively
E xecute	Complete action with commitment	Avoid hesitation

Situational Pressure Management

Situation	Quick reset	Focus cue	Action plan
Service pressure (23-24)	touch shoes → breathe	"Same serve, new point"	Execute routine serve to weakness
Critical pass	clap → shake arms	"Platform ready"	Lower, stable, target setter
Championship point	team huddle → eye contact	"This moment"	Trust preparation, execute
After error	turn away → reset	"Next play mentality"	Immediate refocus routine

Building Confidence Under Pressure

Confidence in volleyball develops like any skill—through progressive challenge and consistent success. Understanding confidence sources helps you maintain it when stakes are high:

Confidence Sources

- **Preparation confidence:** trust in practice quality and volume
- **Physical confidence:** belief in technical skill execution
- **Emotional confidence:** faith in pressure response abilities
- **Social confidence:** trust in teammates and system
- **Strategic confidence:** belief in tactical decision-making

Confidence Development Progression

- **Foundation:** success in controlled practice environments
- **Challenge:** incremental pressure introduction
- **Application:** competitive situation mastery
- **Integration:** automatic confidence response under any pressure

Players who systematically build confidence through this progression show 40% better serving accuracy and 35% higher attack efficiency during championship points.

COMMUNICATION SYSTEMS FOR COMPETITION

Effective On-Court Communication

Communication in volleyball functions like technical execution; it requires practice, timing, and adjustment based on the situation.

Communication Timing

- **Pre-play:** strategic calls, encouragement, system reminders
- **During-play:** ball calls, coverage assignments, adjustments
- **Post-play:** quick feedback, reset cues, energy management
- **Between-points:** brief strategic adjustments, momentum management

Communication Clarity Principles

- **Brevity:** short, clear messages
- **Specificity:** exact information needed
- **Timing:** appropriate message delivery moment
- **Tone:** energy and intent matching situation
- **Consistency:** reliable terminology across situations

Game Communication Playbook

Momentum Builders

- "Great dig, now transition!"
- "Perfect read on that play!"

- "Let's go—our turn!"
- "That's the energy we need!"

Refocus Statements

- "Reset—next play."
- "Stay with the system."
- "Breathe and execute."
- "Back to our game!"

Tactical Adjustments

- "Watch the seam between 3 and 4!"
- "Setter's going quick to middle!"
- "Press the block on this rotation!"
- "Short serve coming—be ready!"

Critical Moment Communication

- "Big point—trust each other!"
- "Execute what we practiced!"
- "This is our moment!"
- "Aggressive but controlled!"

Teams that maintain communication quality throughout close matches win approximately 65% of those matches compared to teams whose communication deteriorates under pressure.

LEADERSHIP DEVELOPMENT IN VOLLEYBALL

Types of Volleyball Leadership
Leadership in volleyball comes in various forms, each valuable to team success. Every team needs a mix of leadership styles to be successful.

Task Leadership
- technical instruction and guidance
- system implementation and adjustment
- performance standard maintenance
- skill development facilitation

Social Leadership
- team chemistry development
- conflict resolution management
- motivation and energy regulation
- inclusive culture creation

Emotional Leadership
- pressure situation management
- confidence building and maintenance
- error response modeling
- resilience demonstration

Leadership Action Plan
Daily Leadership Actions
- Be first in/last out at practice.

- Encourage at least three teammates per session.
- Ask one solution-focused question in team meetings.
- Model perfect practice intensity.

Weekly Leadership Goals
- Attend one extra skills session.
- Review game film and share observations.
- Check in with each teammate personally.
- Lead one team-building activity.

Monthly Leadership Review
- Assess team culture and energy.
- Identify leadership development areas.
- Seek feedback from coaches/teammates.
- Adjust leadership approach as needed.

Situational Leadership

Just as technical execution adapts to different game situations, leadership approach must flex based on team needs:

Leading During Success
- Maintain humility and perspective.
- Keep team focused on next challenge.
- Reinforce positive behaviors and systems.
- Share credit and celebrate collectively.

Leading During Adversity
- Provide emotional stability and calm.

- Focus on process rather than results.
- Encourage solution-focused thinking.
- Demonstrate resilience through action.

Leading in Transitions

- Guide adaptation to new challenges.
- Maintain core values during change.
- Support teammates through uncertainty.
- Bridge individual and team development.

Situational leaders demonstrate 50% better team cohesion during difficult matches and contribute to 30% higher win rates in close games.

GOAL SETTING AND PROGRESS TRACKING

Smart Goal Framework for Volleyball

Like technical progressions, mental development requires specific, measurable targets:

Individual Performance Goals

- **Specific:** "Improve serving accuracy to 85%."
- **Measurable:** tracks serves in practice and games
- **Achievable:** based on current performance levels
- **Relevant:** supports team success and personal development
- **Time-bound:** "by end of season" or specific dates

Performance Tracking Template

Weekly Performance Review

Skill area	Target	Actual	Trend	Next week focus
Serving	80% in-court	78%	↗	Target weak passers
Passing	2.0 average	1.8	↔	Platform stability
Attacking	40% kill %	35%	↗	Shot selection
Blocking	3+ touches/set	2.5	↗	Timing vs. quick

Monthly Development Goals

- **Technical:** one specific skill improvement
- **Physical:** fitness or strength benchmark
- **Mental:** one mental skill mastery
- **Tactical:** system understanding advancement
- **Leadership:** one team impact goal

Team Goal Integration

Mental development supports team objectives through aligned goal-setting:

Collective Goal Categories

- **Performance goals:** win percentage, statistical targets
- **Process goals:** system execution quality, communication standards
- **Development goals:** individual player improvement plans
- **Culture goals:** team chemistry and behavioral standards

Mental Training Techniques
Visualization for Volleyball

Like technical skill practice, visualization strengthens neural pathways for optimal performance:

Technical Visualization

- See/feel perfect skill execution.
- Include all sensory details (sounds, feelings).
- Practice error correction in visualization.
- Rehearse competition scenarios.

Tactical Visualization

- Review game plans and systems.
- Anticipate opponent adjustments.
- Practice decision-making scenarios.
- Visualize successful competition moments.

Visualization Script Template

- **Pre-practice visualization (3 minutes):** "I see myself entering the gym with energy and focus. I feel my body warming up successfully. I visualize executing my primary skills with confidence and precision. I see myself supporting teammates and maintaining positive energy throughout practice."
- **Pre-match visualization (5 minutes):** "I imagine stepping onto the court feeling prepared and confident. I

see myself executing our game plan effectively. I feel my breathing staying calm under pressure. I visualize successful rallies and strong team connections. I see us celebrating success and responding positively to challenges."

Mindfulness for Athletes

Present-moment awareness enhances performance by eliminating distracting thoughts about past errors or future consequences:

Present-Moment Techniques

- **Breathing awareness:** 4-7-8 breathing pattern
- **Body scanning:** Quick tension identification and release
- **Sensory focus:** Court feeling, sound awareness, visual clarity
- **Thought observation:** Notice without judgment, return to task
- **Acceptance practice:** Acknowledge pressure without resistance

Athletes who practice mindfulness techniques show 20% better focus maintenance during extended rallies and 15% improved decision-making under pressure.

BUILDING TEAM CULTURE

Culture Components

Like offensive systems, team culture requires intentional development and maintenance:

Shared Values

- effort and preparation standards
- communication expectations
- support and accountability balance
- growth mindset principles
- competitive integrity

Ritual and Tradition

- pre-game preparation routines
- victory/defeat processing methods
- recognition and celebration practices
- milestone acknowledgment customs
- legacy building activities

Culture Building Checklist

Daily Habits

- ☐ Greet each teammate personally.
- ☐ Share one positive observation.
- ☐ Ask for help when needed.
- ☐ Offer assistance proactively.
- ☐ End practice with team connection.

Weekly Practices

- ☐ Have a team meal or gathering.
- ☐ Conduct a video review session with open discussion.
- ☐ Initiate individual check-ins with key teammates.
- ☐ Celebrate weekly improvements.
- ☐ Conduct a collective goal progress review.

Monthly Culture Reinforcement

- ☐ Have a culture discussion and feedback.
- ☐ Rotate leadership opportunities.
- ☐ Participate in an external team-building activity.
- ☐ Listen to a guest speaker or have a mentor session.
- ☐ Reassess season goals.

IF YOU ONLY REMEMBER ONE THING ABOUT MENTAL PERFORMANCE...

- **Routine creates reliability**: Consistent mental routines produce consistent physical performance.
- **Pressure is privilege**: Reframe pressure situations as opportunities to showcase preparation.
- **Communication is leadership**: How you communicate under pressure defines team culture.
- **Process over outcome**: Focus on execution quality rather than score results.
- **Mental reps matter**: Visualization and mental practice strengthen performance as much as physical practice.

FROM PRACTICE TO PERFORMANCE: MENTAL GAME INTEGRATION

Progressive Mental Training

Mental skills develop through the same progressive approach as physical abilities:

- **Awareness:** Recognize mental patterns and responses.
- **Practice:** Develop mental skills in controlled environments.
- **Application:** Use mental tools in competitive situations.
- **Adaptation:** Adjust mental strategies based on effectiveness.
- **Integration:** Make mental skills automatic responses.

Mental Performance Indicators

Track mental development through observable performance markers:

Individual Indicators

- consistent performance across varying circumstances
- quick recovery from mistakes
- effective pressure management
- clear tactical decision-making
- positive influence on team energy

Team Indicators

- maintained systems under pressure
- strong communication in critical moments
- collective resilience after setbacks

- strategic adaptation during matches
- positive culture sustainability

Research shows that teams with structured mental training programs demonstrate 20-25% better performance in pressure situations and win approximately 60% of close matches compared to teams without mental skills emphasis.

"Mental toughness is not something you're born with. It's developed point by point, error by error, match by match."

The mental game represents volleyball's final frontier—where physical skills meet psychological preparedness to create championship performance. By developing these mental tools systematically, you transform not just your volleyball but your approach to any high-pressure situation in life.

Your mental development journey parallels your technical growth: awareness leads to practice, practice creates competency, and competency breeds the confidence that allows you to perform freely when everything's on the line. The difference between good players and great ones often comes down to who can maintain their technical execution when the mental pressure is highest.

As you integrate these mental skills, you'll discover they enhance every aspect of your game—from serving under pressure to leading teammates through adversity. More importantly, these psychological tools transfer to academic challenges, work situations, and personal relationships long after your playing days conclude.

The final chapter explores the abundant pathways available to continue your volleyball journey, whether through competitive play, coaching, or alternative involvement in the sport you've grown to love.

CHAPTER 10:

BEYOND THE BASICS-PATHWAYS FORWARD

Volleyball is not just a sport—it's a lifelong journey that opens doors you never knew existed.

The final whistle blows on your youth volleyball career. But rather than an ending, this moment marks a thrilling beginning—the launch point for countless opportunities in volleyball's diverse ecosystem. Whether you dream of college scholarships, professional aspirations, coaching youth teams, or simply maintaining volleyball as a lifelong passion, the pathways forward are as varied as they are exciting.

Having mastered the fundamentals through mental game development explored in previous chapters, you now face an exciting question: How will volleyball continue to shape your future? This chapter provides the roadmap for navigating post-youth volleyball opportunities, from immediate next steps to long-term career pathways.

DEVELOPMENT PATHWAY CHECKLIST

Immediate Opportunities

☐ Identify local club and travel team options.

☐ Research volleyball camps and clinics in your area.

☐ Connect with high school coaching staff.

☐ Begin tracking personal statistics and video.

☐ Establish relationships with college programs of interest.

Medium-Term Development

☐ Create athletic resume with achievements.

☐ Develop highlight video for recruiting.

☐ Research college volleyball programs and requirements.

☐ Consider specialized position training.

☐ Explore beach volleyball opportunities.

Long-Term Pathways

☐ Understand college volleyball recruiting timeline.

☐ Research post-college playing opportunities.

☐ Explore volleyball-related career paths.

☐ Plan for coaching certification if interested.

☐ Maintain volleyball network connections.

Lifelong Engagement

☐ Consider recreational league participation.

☐ Explore volleyball teaching opportunities.

☐ Stay connected to volleyball community.

☐ Support youth development programs.

☐ Maintain personal fitness through volleyball.

WHAT YOU CAN DO THIS MONTH

Activity	Purpose	How to start
Research three college programs	Build knowledge of options	Visit team websites, watch matches online
Reach out to one coach	Begin relationships	Send introduction email with basic stats
Start your highlight reel	Prepare recruiting materials	Collect game footage, identify best plays
Help coach a local 10U team	Develop teaching skills	Contact local club about volunteer opportunities
Play beach one weekend	Expand volleyball versatility	Find local beach courts, organize small group

COLLEGE VOLLEYBALL PATHWAY

Understanding College Volleyball Levels

Just as you progressed through skill levels in youth volleyball, college volleyball offers distinct competitive tiers, each with unique opportunities:

NCAA Division I

- highest competitive level
- full scholarship opportunities
- year-round training commitment
- national championship competition
- significant time demands (20+ hours/week)

NCAA Division II

- high competitive level
- partial scholarship opportunities
- competitive season with championship tournaments
- balanced academic and athletic focus
- regional competition emphasis

NCAA Division III

- competitive level without athletic scholarships
- strong academic-athletic balance
- conference championships and tournaments
- excellent development opportunities
- merit-based financial aid available

Junior College (JUCO)

- two-year competitive programs
- full and partial scholarships available
- transfer pathway to four-year programs
- intensive playing experience
- academic and athletic development

College Recruiting Timeline

Understanding recruiting timing prevents missed opportunities and overwhelming rush toward deadlines:

Grade level	Focus areas	Key actions
Freshman	Skill development, academic foundation	Join club team, attend camps, build GPA
Sophomore	Competition experience, position specialization	Create athletic profile, attend showcases
Junior	Recruiting preparation, program research	Send letters to coaches, unofficial visits
Senior	Official visits, decision making	Complete applications, NCAA paperwork

College Recruiting Process

Success in college recruiting requires the same systematic approach you've learned in volleyball skill development:

Creating Your Athletic Profile

- **Athletic resume:** statistics, honors, team achievements
- **Highlight video:** 5–7 minutes showcasing best plays
- **Academic transcript:** GPA and test scores
- **Character references:** coaches, teachers, mentors
- **Contact information:** updated regularly

College Coach Communication

- Send initial inquiry emails with highlights.
- Follow up after showcases/tournaments.
- Update progress throughout seasons.
- Express genuine interest in programs.
- Maintain professional communication.

Scholarship Considerations

Understanding scholarship structures helps manage expectations and plan financially:

Full vs. Partial Scholarships

- Full scholarships cover tuition, room/board, and books.
- Partial scholarships may cover portions of expenses.
- Academic scholarships can supplement athletic aid.
- Need-based aid is often available alongside athletic aid.

NCAA Scholarship Limits

- **Division I:** 12 full scholarships per team
- **Division II:** 8 full scholarships per team
- **JUCO:** varies by conference and scholarship type

Note: Scholarship availability varies significantly by program competitiveness, conference strength, and individual player marketability.

ADVANCED TRAINING OPPORTUNITIES

Specialized Position Training

Just as you've developed position-specific skills, advanced training opportunities offer deeper specialization:

Position-Specific Camps

- setter-focused skill development
- middle blocker specialized training
- libero/defensive specialist camps
- beach volleyball transition training

- position-specific technique refinement

Professional Volleyball Camps
- national training centers
- Olympic Training Center programs
- professional club training camps
- international development programs
- elite athlete showcases

Beach Volleyball Development
Beach volleyball represents a distinct pathway requiring adapted skills:

Beach vs. Indoor Transition
- two-person team dynamics
- specialized skills (hand setting rules)
- weather condition training
- sand-specific movement patterns
- tournament circuit participation

Beach Volleyball Opportunities
- college beach volleyball programs
- professional beach tours (AVL, NVL)
- international beach volleyball
- Olympic pathway programs
- regional and national championships

Many successful indoor players enhance their overall volleyball understanding through beach experience, developing superior court awareness and refined ball control skills.

VOLLEYBALL CAREER PATHWAYS

Playing Professionally
Professional volleyball opportunities exist across multiple levels and geographic regions:

International Professional Volleyball
- European leagues (Italy, Poland, Russia)
- Asian leagues (Japan, Korea, China)
- Brazilian Superliga
- seasonal contracts and opportunities

Semi-Professional Opportunities
- Athletes Unlimited Volleyball
- club-level competitive leagues
- regional professional tournaments
- exhibition and showcase events

Coaching Career Development

Coaching provides a natural transition for passionate volleyball players:

Coaching Certification Pathway

1. **USAV Certification Levels:**
   - o CAP I: Recreational coaching
   - o CAP II: Junior club coaching
   - o CAP III: Advanced club coaching
   - o CAP IV: Elite coaching certification
2. **Coaching Development Options:**
   - o Assistant coach positions
   - o Club team volunteer coaching
   - o School program involvement
   - o Camps and clinics instruction
   - o Mentorship under experienced coaches

Volleyball-Related Careers

Your volleyball experience creates transferable skills valuable in numerous industries:

Sports Industry Opportunities

- athletic training and sports medicine
- sports journalism and broadcasting
- event management and tournament direction
- volleyball equipment design and sales
- facility management and operations

Educational Pathways
- physical education teaching
- kinesiology and exercise science
- sports psychology specialization
- athletic administration
- sports marketing and promotion

Continuing Education
- USAV coaching education programs
- volleyball-specific certifications
- sports science degree programs
- annual coaching conferences
- online coaching education platforms

VOLLEYBALL COMMUNITY ENGAGEMENT

Building Your Volleyball Network

Like building team chemistry, creating professional networks requires intentional effort:

Networking Strategies
- **Stay connected with coaches:** Maintain relationships with youth coaches, connect with college coaching staff, and engage with club directors.
- **Alumni connections:** Join volleyball alumni groups, attend program reunions, mentor younger players, and support current team activities.

- **Professional associations:** Join coaching associations, participate in volleyball organizations, attend industry conferences, and engage in volleyball forums.

Giving Back to the Sport

Your volleyball journey includes the responsibility to support future generations:

Volunteer Opportunities

- youth program assistant coaching
- tournament volunteer work
- clinic instruction and demonstration
- mentoring young players
- community league coaching

Community Impact

- Start volleyball programs in underserved areas.
- Donate equipment to youth programs.
- Sponsor local teams or players.
- Host volleyball clinics and camps.

LONG-TERM ATHLETIC DEVELOPMENT PLAN

Creating Your 5-Year Volleyball Vision

Strategic planning helps navigate the transition from youth to adult volleyball involvement:

Year 1–2 Goals

- skill refinement and specialization
- competitive team experience
- academic excellence maintenance
- college program identification

Year 3–4 Goals

- college volleyball decision
- advanced skill development
- leadership role assumption
- career pathway exploration

Year 5+ Vision

- post-college playing decisions
- professional development pursuit
- community engagement planning
- lifelong volleyball involvement

Personal Development Integration

Balancing volleyball with comprehensive life development ensures sustainable long-term success:

Balancing Volleyball With Life

- academic achievement emphasis
- career skill development
- social relationship maintenance
- financial planning consideration
- health and wellness priorities

MY VOLLEYBALL LEGACY STATEMENT

"I will keep growing, give back when I can, and carry the lessons of this game into every part of my life."

Your volleyball legacy extends beyond personal statistics and accomplishments. Consider how your journey will impact the future of the sport and those who follow you. This statement serves as your commitment to remain part of the volleyball community while applying its lessons throughout your life.

Legacy Components

- skills and knowledge you'll share with others
- leadership qualities you'll bring to future endeavors
- commitment to volleyball's continued growth
- application of volleyball lessons to life challenges
- support for future volleyball generations

IF YOU ONLY REMEMBER ONE THING ABOUT YOUR VOLLEYBALL FUTURE...

- **Stay connected to the game**: Volleyball offers lifelong opportunities for growth, connection, and joy.
- **Keep developing**: Your volleyball journey can continue to evolve in countless directions.
- **Pay it forward**: Use your experience to help develop the next generation of players.
- **Embrace the journey**: Success in volleyball comes in many forms beyond playing.
- **Maintain perspective**: Volleyball is a vehicle for life lessons and lasting relationships.

FROM YOUTH TO LIFELONG VOLLEYBALL

The Journey Continues

Your youth volleyball experience has provided foundational skills extending far beyond athletic achievement. The discipline, teamwork, and resilience developed through volleyball create a framework for lifelong success—whether you pursue competitive athletics, professional careers, or maintain volleyball as a cherished hobby.

Creating Your Volleyball Future

Immediate Next Steps

1. **Reflect on tour experience:** Identify greatest volleyball achievements, recognize personal growth, and acknowledge relationships made, celebrate challenges overcome.

2. **Set future intentions:** Determine desired involvement level, identify specific pathways, research available opportunities, and create realistic action plans.

3. **Stay engaged:** Maintain volleyball community connections, seek new opportunities, share knowledge with others, and continue skill development.

The Ripple Effect

Your volleyball journey creates impact beyond personal development. Every skill mastered, leadership lesson learned, and relationship built contributes to volleyball's evolving community. Consider how your continued involvement might do the following:

- inspire young players entering the sport
- support teammates throughout their journeys
- honor coaches who shaped your development
- strengthen the broader volleyball community
- create opportunities for future generations

THE ONGOING ADVENTURE

Rather than concluding your volleyball story, this handbook's final chapter marks your transition into volleyball's broader landscape. Whether pursuing collegiate athletics, coaching careers, professional opportunities, or recreational involvement, your volleyball foundation prepares you for continued growth.

The skills you've developed—discipline, teamwork, resilience, communication, and leadership—transcend sport, preparing you for success in any chosen path. Volleyball has been your training ground for life's challenges and opportunities.

Resources for Your Journey

- USAV (USA Volleyball) website and programs
- local volleyball clubs and organizations
- college volleyball team websites
- professional volleyball league information
- volleyball coaching and education resources

As you transition beyond youth volleyball, remember that your story continues writing itself across experiences yet to come. The court awaits whenever you need it—for fitness, friendship, stress relief, or simply the joy of executing perfect technique you've spent years developing.

Your volleyball journey represents one thread in the sport's vast tapestry—a continuum spanning from community recreation to Olympic competition. By staying connected to volleyball, you ensure this transformative sport continues enriching your life while contributing to others' development.

The skills, relationships, and lessons gained through volleyball will serve you throughout life. Whether you compete professionally, coach future champions, or enjoy weekly pickup games, volleyball remains a source of challenge, connection, and personal growth.

Welcome to volleyball's extended family—a global community united by a shared understanding of this beautiful, challenging sport. Your competitive youth career concludes, but your volleyball journey evolves into whatever directions bring you joy and purpose.

The final serve of your youth volleyball career simultaneously represents your first serve in volleyball's lifelong game.

CONCLUSION:
THE VOLLEYBALL JOURNEY

The volleyball journey never truly ends—it evolves, deepens, and continues to offer new lessons and opportunities throughout life. From those first awkward attempts to simply get the ball over the net to mastering complex systems and leading teammates through pressure-filled moments, you've developed not just athletic skills but life skills that will serve you forever.

Every great setter began with imperfect hands-on first contact. Every powerful attacker started with an uncoordinated approach to footwork. Every defensive specialist learned to dive for balls they once thought unreachable. Your journey reflects this same progression—from uncertainty to competence, from individual focus to team leadership, from simply playing the game to understanding its deeper lessons.

Volleyball has taught you that success comes from preparation, that resilience builds from repeated challenge, that leadership emerges from service to others, and that individual excellence means little without collective achievement. These aren't just volleyball lesson; they're blueprints for approaching any challenge life presents.

As you move forward, whether toward college volleyball, coaching future generations, or maintaining volleyball as a cherished hobby, you carry with you a unique perspective. You understand that the path to excellence is built on fundamentals executed consistently, that systems and teamwork triumph over individual heroics, and that mental strength often determines outcomes more than physical gifts.

Most importantly, you've learned that volleyball is about connection—the connection between individual skills and team success, between preparation and performance, between coaching wisdom and player growth, and ultimately between people who share this beautiful, challenging, ever-evolving sport.

Your volleyball story doesn't end with youth leagues or even college—it transforms. You become part of a continuum, passing knowledge to those who follow, drawing inspiration from those who came before, and contributing to a sport that has given you so much.

The skills you've mastered, the relationships you've forged, and the lessons you've learned have prepared you not just for volleyball success but for life success. As you serve this final point in your youth volleyball journey, remember that it's also your first serve in the broader game of life.

Thank you for being part of the volleyball community. The court is always there when you need it, and somewhere, another young player is just beginning their journey, perhaps holding this same handbook, taking their first steps toward the same transformative experience you've completed.

The path to volleyball excellence, as you now know, is paved with consistency, built on fundamentals, strengthened by teamwork, and elevated by leadership.

Your journey continues. The next serve is yours.

REFERENCES

- American Volleyball Coaches Association. (2022). *AVCA volleyball skill development guide* (4th ed.). AVCA.
- Belyaev, A. V., & Bulykina, L. V. (2021). Modern approaches to the volleyball teaching process for young athletes. *Journal of Human Sport and Exercise, 16*(2), 392-401. https://doi.org/10.14198/jhse.2021.162.09
- Bompa, T. O., & Buzzichelli, C. A. (2019). *Periodization: Theory and methodology of training* (6th ed.). Human Kinetics.
- Buckner, S. L., Jessee, M. B., & Dankel, S. J. (2020). The basics of training for muscle size and strength: A review for those with limited time and facilities. *Sports Medicine, 50*(10), 1821-1834. https://doi.org/10.1007/s40279-020-01331-7
- Ciuffarella, A., Russo, L., Masedu, F., Valenti, M., Izzo, R. E., & De Angelis, M. (2023). Notational analysis of the volleyball serve: A systematic review. *Sports Medicine, 53*(7), 1429-1451. https://doi.org/10.1007/s40279-023-01789-1

- Gardner, H., & Kirby, J. (2022). *The coach's playbook: Developing team culture in volleyball* (2nd ed.). Championship Productions.
- Haff, G. G., & Triplett, N. T. (Eds.). (2021). *Essentials of strength training and conditioning* (4th ed.). Human Kinetics.
- International Volleyball Federation. (2023). *Official volleyball rules 2023-2024.* FIVB.
- Kiraly, K., & Shewman, B. (2019). *Championship volleyball techniques and drills* (3rd ed.). Human Kinetics.
- Lenberg, K. (2021). *Volleyball skills & drills* (5th ed.). Human Kinetics.
- Marques Junior, N. K. (2020). Decision-making in volleyball: A systematic review. *International Journal of Human Movement and Sports Sciences, 8*(3), 100-109. https://doi.org/10.13189/saj.2020.080305
- McGown, C., Fronske, H., & Moser, L. (2020). *Coaching volleyball: Building a winning team* (5th ed.). Routledge.
- Moran, A. P. (2018). *The psychology of concentration in sport performers: A cognitive analysis* (2nd ed.). Psychology Press.
- NCAA. (2023). *2023-24 NCAA Division I manual.* National Collegiate Athletic Association.
- Reeser, J. C., & Bahr, R. (Eds.). (2022). *Volleyball sports medicine and science* (2nd ed.). Springer.
- Reynaud, C. (2021). *The volleyball coaching bible, volume II.* Human Kinetics.
- Samozino, P., Rejc, E., Di Prampero, P. E., Belli, A., & Morin, J. B. (2022). Optimal force-velocity profile in ballistic movements: Altius: Citius or Fortius? *Medicine &*

Science in Sports & Exercise, 44(2), 313-322. https://doi.org/10.1249/MSS.0b013e31822d757a

- Stone, M. H., Stone, M., & Sands, W. A. (2019). *Principles and practice of resistance training.* Human Kinetics.

- Valenzuela, P. L., Montero-Rodríguez, C., & Menéndez, H. (2023). Training load, well-being and performance in volleyball: A systematic review. *Journal of Sports Science and Medicine, 22*(2), 183-194.

- USA Volleyball. (2023). *USA Volleyball coaching accreditation program manual* (2023-2024). USA Volleyball.

- Weinberg, R. S., & Gould, D. (2023). *Foundations of sport and exercise psychology* (8th ed.). Human Kinetics.

- Williams, J. M., & Krane, V. (2021). *Applied sport psychology: Personal growth to peak performance* (8th ed.). McGraw-Hill Education.

- Wise, M. (2020). *Coaching volleyball: Techniques and tactical skills* (4th ed.). Human Kinetics.

www.ingramcontent.com/pod-product-compliance
Lightning Source LLC
Chambersburg PA
CBHW061148120626
46546CB00005B/1969